Methuen Studies in Science

Nature Conservation

A PRACTICAL HANDBOOK

W. M. M. BARON B.Sc., M.A., F.L.S.

Head of the Science Department
Winchester College

Methuen Educational Ltd

LONDON · TORONTO · SYDNEY · WELLINGTON

Methuen Studies in Science

GENERAL EDITOR   J. M. Gregory M.A., D.Phil., Winchester College

CONSULTANT EDITORS   B. E. Dawson B.Sc., Ph.D., King's College, London

                       R. Gliddon B.Sc., Ph.D., Clifton College, Bristol

Nature Conservation	W. M. M. Baron
Chemical Equilibrium	J. S. Coe
Enzymes	Alan D. B. Malcolm
Energy in Chemistry	B. E. Dawson
Alternating Currents	J. M. Gregory
Logical Control Systems	Keith Morphew
Aspects of Isomerism	Peter Uzzell
The Inorganic Chemistry of the Non-metals	John Emsley
Atomic and Molecular Weight Determination	R. B. Moyes
The Mechanical Properties of Materials	R. A. Farrar

Forthcoming	
The States of Matter	A. Ralph Morgan
Oscillations	Ian B. Hopley
Transition Metal Chemistry	Jeff Thompson
Crystals and their Structures	I. F. Roberts
Catalysis in Chemistry	A. J. B. Robertson
Molecular Spectroscopy	Aline Bradshaw
Kinetics and Mechanisms of Reactions	B. E. Dawson
Waves	Ian B. Hopley
Radioisotopes	D. J. Hornsey
Fundamental Electrostatics	S. W. Hockey

First published 1971
by Methuen Educational Ltd
11 New Fetter Lane, London EC4
© 1971 by W. M. M. Baron
Printed in Great Britain by
William Clowes & Sons Ltd.,
London, Colchester and Beccles

SBN 423 79960 6 non net
    423 84290 0 net

Preface

There is now a widespread interest in conservation and a growing conviction that the various problems of natural and economic resources, population, pollution and recreation must be solved within the next few decades. In some ways our time may be running out; perhaps we have another ten years to organise ourselves and our resources, on a global scale, otherwise by the beginning of the next century we will be in for a catastrophe more chilling in scale at least than anything we have had to contend with in the course of history.

It is all very fine though to preach global conservation; while public opinion is vital in helping to sway the opinion of politicians and planners, there is still a very real need for many of us to do something active and constructive to help keep our country a healthy place to live in. Not just healthy in an unpolluted sense, but healthy in an aesthetic and emotionally satisfying way. Modern town conservation and planning involves much of this ideal but the aim of this book is almost entirely towards nature conservation. Clearly this is only one facet of the whole conservation movement yet one of particular importance as it is in the country that people can obtain both the relaxation and stimulus that have become particularly vital as a change from life in town and city. It is most often in the country that one can experience a sense of exploration and be struck by the unexpectedness of new natural situations.

My approach to the problems of nature conservation has been mostly restricted to my own experience in the southern part of England. In many ways this has been quite deliberate as I believe that it can only be by showing in detail how certain management problems have been solved that there can be any useful impact in this kind of work.

Winchester

W.M.M.B.

Acknowledgements

I am most grateful to the following for allowing me to make use of their photographs: the Esso Petroleum Company for Figs. 3, 6 and 7; the Town Clerk of the Borough of Basingstoke, Messrs. Lemon and Blizard and Southern Air Photos for Fig. 4; C. C. Bonsey and the Royal Commission on Historical Monuments for Figs. 8 and 9; J. K. S. St. Joseph and the Cambridge University Collection for Fig. 15; Dr. M. C. F. Proctor for Fig. 16; The Reindeer Company and David Stephens for Fig. 18; The Scots Magazine for Fig. 20; Nicholas Meyjes and The Field for Fig. 24; G. A. Walsh and The Hampshire Chronicle for Fig. 31; H. A. G. Blackwell for Fig. 34; Frank Lundgren for Fig. 37. I am also grateful to J. F. Barrow for providing me with details of the South Hampshire Plan; the Institute of Biology and Dr. E. J. Wilkins for the details in Tables 1 and 2; various pupils, particularly N. J. E. Harrison and J. D. McMillan for putting together the information in Fig. 10; M. Bryant for his assistance with Tables 7 and 9; Dr. P. Merrett and the Zoological Society of London for the data in Fig. 12; The British Trust for Ornithology for the details in Table 12; my pupil R. J. A. Tulloch for the work carried out on the mammals in the Fallodon Nature Reserve. I owe particular thanks to the Nature Conservancy for their help and for allowing me to make use of details in the map of the Cairngorms National Nature Reserve and the Loch an Eilein Nature Trail Guides, and I am grateful to the Ordnance Survey and the Controller of H.M. Stationery Office for allowing me to use a map of the area.

I would also like to take the opportunity of particularly thanking C. C. Bonsey and G. V. Darrah for their help and advice, M. R. Stanley-Price for reading the manuscript and helping me in numerous ways, and finally Mrs. K. J. Tewkesbury for her infinite patience in preparing the typescript.

Contents

Bibliography

ARVILL, R. *Man and Environment.* Penguin, 1969

ASHBY, M. *Plant Ecology.* Macmillan, 1961

BARR, J. *Derelict Britain.* Penguin, 1969

BRIERLEY, J. K. *Biology and the Social Crisis.* Heinemann, 1967

BRIERLEY, J. K. *A Natural History of Man.* Heinemann, 1970

CAIRNGORM AREA. *Report of the Technical Group.* Scottish Development Dept.,
    Edinburgh, 1967

CALDER, N. *Technopolis: Social Control of the Uses of Science.* MacGibbon and Kee, 1969

CARSON, R. *The Silent Spring.* Hamish Hamilton, 1963

CONSERVATION SOCIETY. *Why Britain Needs a Population Policy.* Conservation Society,
    Potters Bar, Hertford, 1969

DARLINGTON, A. *Ecology of Refuse Tips.* Heinemann, 1969

DASMAN, R. F. *Environmental Conservation.* Wiley, New York, 1970

DONALDSON, J. G. S., DONALDSON, F. and BARBER, D. *Farming in Britain Today.*
    Penguin, 1969

DOWDESWELL, W. H. *Animal Ecology.* Methuen, 1959

DOWDESWELL, W. H. *Practical Animal Ecology.* Methuen, 1959

EHRLICH, P. R. and EHRLICH, A. H. *Population: Resources: Environment.* Freeman, San
    Francisco, 1970

FISHER, J., SIMON, N. and VINCENT, J. *The Red Book.* Collins, 1969

FRASER DARLING, F. *Wilderness and Plenty.* Reith Lectures, BBC, 1969

FROST, W. E. and BROWN, M. E. *The Trout.* New Naturalist Series, Collins, 1967

GRISMEK, B. *Serengeti Shall not Die.* Collins, 1960

H.R.H. THE DUKE OF EDINBURGH and FISHER, J. *Wildlife Crisis.* Hamish Hamilton, 1970

LINDGREN, E. J. *The Herd of Reindeer.* Glenmore: Cairngorms Forest Park Guide, HMSO,
    Edinburgh, 1966

LOWRY, J. H. *World Population and Food Supply.* Arnold, 1970

MELLANBY, K. *Pesticides and Pollution.* New Naturalist Series, Collins, 1967

MORRIS, D. *The Human Zoo.* Jonathan Cape, 1969

NICHOLSON, E. M. *Britain's Nature Reserves.* Country Life, 1957

NICHOLSON, E. M. *The Environmental Revolution.* Hodder and Stoughton, 1970

PRIME, C. T. *Investigations in Woodland Ecology.* Heinemann, 1970

STAMP, Sir D. *Nature Conservation in Britain.* New Naturalist Series, Collins, 1969

STREET, P. *Vanishing Animals; Preserving Nature's Rarities.* Faber and Faber, 1961

TAYLOR, L. R. (Editor). *The Optimum Population of Britain.* Institute of Biology Symposium,
    1969

VERNON, B. 'Towards a Family Planning Service.' *Municipal Review*, **40**, 248-250, May 1969

WILSON, R. W. 'Conservation in School Science Courses.' *School Science Review*, **168**, 420

YAPP, W. B. (Editor). *The Effects of Pollution on Living Material.* Institute of Biology
    Symposium, 1959

1 Conservation:
a statement of the problems

The aims of conservation

Ever since he first evolved, man has been involved with some degree of struggle with his environment for his survival. But during the last few decades he has come to regard the environment as something he can overcome or tame, and in doing so has forgotten that he himself is part of what we used to call Nature: of the global ecosystem. Gradually, however, people are beginning to realise that this attitude is dangerous and likely to result in serious calamity unless we think again. Conservation is essentially the taking care of our environment so that it may continue to be a fit place for living things. It is by no means a new concept but it is only recently that it has become an everyday household word. The popularity of the concept of conservation is the result of our overdue awareness of the serious environmental problems which have been created by careless exploitation of natural resources and increasing population with its ancillary effects.

Increasing population means more houses and roads, more factories to work in and a more technological agriculture to provide the necessary food. The resulting demand for land inevitably reduces the amount of unspoiled country, country which is now receiving more holiday visitors than ever before. We have been told of the necessity of increasing our gross national product, of the importance of economic growth, yet all countries are of limited size and growth cannot continue indefinitely. How are we to achieve an ecological stability? Perhaps for the first time in man's existence he not only can see and partly understand the problems, but he has the technological capacity to cope with the situation. The problems are not only economic but educational, sociological and political.

Planning for the future

The planners are fully aware of these problems and 'planning for the year 2000' is becoming a fascinating and very real activity, with most County Councils making serious efforts to plan for the future. An illustration of this is the work being carried out in Hampshire by the County Council who are trying to predict and plan for a given growth rate. The South Hampshire plan covers an area of considerable natural beauty with chalk downland, chalk streams, marshes and woodland as well as the two large cities of Portsmouth and Southampton. The population of this area is about 890,000 (1970) and it is predicted that this will increase at the rate of 13,000 to 14,000 per year, about half of which growth is due to internal growth and half to immigration from other parts of the country. The graph below (Fig. 1) illustrates how the population of the area is predicted to change towards the year 2000.

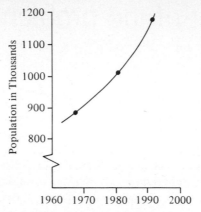

Fig. 1. Population of the South Hampshire area

Unless legislation is brought in to prevent such growth, plans must be made to cater for it in the best possible way. The chart below summarises some of the effects which can be actively planned for:

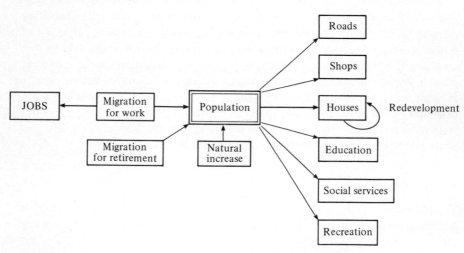

Employment itself will be a problem. Work for some 122,000 should be available through normal industrial growth, but much of this will be in office jobs, and in the more technical industries such as electronics. The building of factories will consume a considerable area, probably 2 square kilometres by 1981 and the same again by 1991.

Housing is a major difficulty; by 1991, 148,000 new houses will be needed and 140,000 existing houses will have to be improved.

What sort of housing should be built? Blocks of flats eat up less land than detached or semi-detached houses, but can often dominate the landscape and, which is more serious, they tend to produce undesirable social consequences. The desire to own (or rent) your own plot of land is a strong and probably innate reaction. It is vital that the right sort of housing should be organised, suitable, as far as one can predict, for the needs of the next twenty or more years.

Both industrial and domestic needs for simple commodities like water will increase proportionately. Water extraction from our rivers and, in the case of Hampshire, the water-bearing strata many hundreds of feet down, cannot continue indefinitely. The delightful river valleys would be the first to suffer but other environmental upsets could well follow. Reservoirs holding water back close to the sea must be constructed, but, again, more land will be consumed. The disposal of sewage and wastes will also increase; modern incinerators and 'composters' to amalgamate sewage with ash waste must be set up. However, as always, the expense is considerable and councils may be reluctant to spend money on these machines when tipping space is still available.

Many more people will be using cars. In 1966, 157,000 cars were on the roads in South Hampshire; by 1991 it will be half a million. This means that we shall have to build more roads and, again, more land will be consumed. Possibilities that may have to be examined are greater control of licences and also more effective use of public transport, particularly in the denser urban areas. The shopping facilities available to the enlarged population must also increase — an area something like four times that currently available in the centre of Southampton will be needed.

Facilities for both young and old will have to be rethought; people will be living longer and education may have to be planned to cover a much wider age range.

All these schemes will absorb a great deal of the countryside. The technical unit of the planners has attempted to grade the land according to both its agricultural and natural history value. In this way it has become possible to suggest the conservation of certain areas while others may be built up as deliberate 'honey-pots' to attract large numbers of visitors. Figure 2 illustrates a typical area of South Hampshire Countryside at Catherington Down, where a small County open space and Nature Reserve has been set up. Historic, archaeological and other sites will also have to be able to cater for more visitors.

Because of all this, the essentially rural picture of much of South Hampshire will have to change radically during the next thirty years; town and country must come closer together and much closer supervision of the whole *community* of the area will be needed if life is to be at all worthwhile.

Nature conservation cannot divorce itself from all this; man is as much a part of the ecosystem as interesting wildlife is. A knowledge of the situation and of the countryside can go a long way towards helping to prevent the worst abuses of

Fig. 2. A view of a South Hampshire Reserve at Catherington Down

mistaken planning; indeed it is one of the aims of this book to show that a personal involvement is not only possible but worthwhile in every way. A greater public awareness of the dangers can do much to influence attitudes, even at a political level.

Pollution

If the planners fail to take all the dangers into account, the growth outlined in this discussion of the South Hampshire plan could lead to a general environmental deterioration. During the last few years there has been abundant evidence of this, the deterioration is not only due to increased building and loss of country, but also to noise disturbance and the wastes of modern life. Indeed it is these unfortunate consequences of the increasingly industrial and technological world that have really served to draw the attention of the public to the conservation movement.

The study and control of the forms of pollution are a vital part of conservation. Sewage effluents, factory waste and smoke from factory and domestic fires all have to be rendered as harmless as possible and dispersed from towns and cities. As technology becomes more sophisticated, new substances and chemicals are used and the effects of these on the environment are often difficult to detect let alone predict for the future. Yet we cannot afford to damage either our own or our neighbours' environment; the world is too small.

Figure 3 shows part of the Solent and the Fawley Marine Terminal of the Esso Petroleum Company. Here industry has taken great trouble to minimise disturbance to the surrounding communities by reducing smell, noise and water pollution. In addition, the visual aspects have been carefully studied so that the building of this

Fig. 3. An aerial view across the Solent of the Fawley Marine Terminal from the south-east, showing the New Forest beyond

vast refinery does not destroy the magnificent views across both the Solent and the New Forest.

AIR POLLUTION   Environmental deterioration is never difficult to find. The atmosphere is frequently hazy with smoke or exhaust fumes. It is even thought that sulphur dioxide, released by modern oil-burning heaters and power stations in Britain, is having some effect on the level of sulphates in Scandinavian soils. Yet in Britain, with the passing of the age of the old-fashioned coal fire, and the Clean Air Act of 1956, the problem of atmospheric pollution is now seldom intense; even so the data in the table below indicates what large amounts may be deposited.

Table 1 Typical results of air pollution measurements in different localities (yearly averages) (after Wilkins, 1959)

	Heavily industrialised	Cities and urban	Rural
Deposited matter (kg/m²/year)			
Grit and dust	0·2–0·4	0·08–0·16	0·02
Dissolved	0·06	0·04	0·02
Sulphur dioxide			
Parts per million by volume	0·10–0·15	0·1	0·01
Smoke (mg/m³)	0·5	0·2–0·5	0·01

This contrasts favourably with parts of America where the atmosphere seems to be perpetually hazy, and where even the photosynthetic efficiency of plant life is sometimes reduced. High-flying aircraft can cause the formation of high altitude cirrus clouds which may reduce the intensity of light falling on plants, and in some cases atmospheric pollution may lead to soot being deposited on the surfaces of leaves. In extreme cases toxic gases may cause the death of the plant.

Exhaust gases from cars and lorries can also be dangerous, particularly in busy built-up areas, though the effect here is mostly on the driver and the city inhabitants. The table below gives the composition of motor vehicle exhaust gases and the toxic limits of concentration for 8 hours' exposure (after Wilkins, 1959).

Table 2

Constituent	Typical concentrations from		Approx. toxic level (p.p.m.)
	Diesel engines (p.p.m.)	Petrol engines (p.p.m.)	
Carbon monoxide	1000	30,000	100
Hydrocarbons	200	500	—
Nitrogen peroxide	400	600	5
Sulphur dioxide	200	60	5

The concentration in a busy London street is seldom more than 20 to 50 p.p.m. of carbon monoxide, but a driver, in more direct contact with the fumes, may get as much as 130 p.p.m. in the air he breathes in. This is likely to cause at least sleepiness and may slow the driver's reactions.

The lead anti-knock compounds in fuels are also giving cause for concern and in some areas have caused a killing off of roadside vegetation. A particularly interesting case occurs in the Los Angeles district of California where the hydrocarbons released in car exhausts combine with the nitrogen peroxide and ozone of the atmosphere under the effect of bright sunshine to produce an irritant tear-inducing fog which is also damaging to plant life. Pine trees in the Californian Sierras over 100 km from Los Angeles are beginning to die from the effects of this pollution.

POLLUTION OF FRESH WATER   Water pollution seems to have a quicker impact on the public. No one wishes to drink foul-tasting water and the recent cases of river poisoning make us all feel particularly vulnerable. The two main causes of fresh water pollution are sewage effluent and agricultural and industrial wastes. All natural rivers and lakes contain decaying organic materials formed by the action of micro-organisms on dead animals and plants. These fungi, bacteria and protozoa absorb oxygen from the water in order to break down these materials and release simple inorganic substances such as phosphates and nitrates. Under natural conditions this is a fair state of affairs as these substances are re-cycled into living things. However, poor or untreated sewage effluents will cause a serious depletion of the dissolved oxygen content of the water and a conspicuous rise in ammonia, phosphate and nitrate. Because of these two factors, higher animal life is greatly reduced, and this results in a bloom of algae. This over-rich state of affairs is called *eutrophication* and is occurring in the Great Lakes of America where so much effluent has poured into them that many of the fish and aquatic animals have died off and some lakes (e.g. parts of Lake Michigan) have been declared unfit for bathing.

Fig. 4. An aerial view of the Sewage Treatment works at Basingstoke, Hampshire

The effective treatment of sewage from a large town or city requires expensive and quite elaborate plant (see Fig. 4) but nowadays in Britain discharge of untreated sewage into our rivers seldom occurs, though it is often discharged into estuaries and the sea. In some cases though, treated or partly treated effluent may be passed into a river. Samples of both the effluent and river water can be taken by the River Authority and, with the dilution factor known, the effects on the biology of the river predicted at least to some extent. Table 3 summarises a sample taken in a recent survey.

Three of these substances are worth examining in more detail: oxygen, simple inorganic ions and other chemicals.

There are two aspects that relate to oxygen availability. Water fully saturated with oxygen at 12°C contains only 7·44 cm³ of the gas per litre. However, water is often super-saturated and figures as high as 130% saturation are sometimes recorded. Most fish are capable of living at as low as 60% saturation. Effluents contain solid and dissolved organic matter and micro-organisms deplete the oxygen as they break

7

Table 3 The concentration of various substances in partly treated sewage effluent and in a good-quality chalk stream, before the arrival of the effluent. The predicted concentrations in the resulting mixture suggest that a toxic level is reached with detergent and that the B.O.D. is also too high.

	Partly treated sewage effluent	River (chalk stream)	1 to 12 mixture
Dissolved oxygen (% saturation)	11	80 (winter)	75
Biochemical oxygen demand (B.O.D.) (p.p.m.) ($20°C$ for 5 days)	142	2–3	12
Ammoniacal nitrogen (p.p.m.)	1·34	none	0·1
Detergents (p.p.m.)	c. 20	none	c. 1·7
Other chemicals		not known	

this down. This can be studied by the Biochemical Oxygen Demand test (B.O.D.) in which a sample is incubated for 5 days at $20°C$ and the oxygen taken up calculated in parts per million, a resulting figure of five being considered high. Ammonia is itself highly toxic and this will also result in a depletion of oxygen as oxidation takes place with the formation of nitrites and nitrates. However, provided the oxygen saturation does not drop below 60% there is no cause for worry, except perhaps when water is low during the summer. Then the ratio of effluent to river flow will increase and at the same time the oxygen saturation will drop with the increase in temperature. At $18°C$ one litre of water contains only $6·54$ cm^3 of oxygen when fully saturated, a conspicuous fall compared with the $12°C$ value. The slower water of summertime will also tend to allow solid detritus to accumulate and this may aggravate the depletion of oxygen in still water areas.

The nitrates, phosphates and other inorganic ions contained in the effluent and released as products of decay are similar to agricultural fertilisers, which may be washed into the river from surrounding agricultural land. These may be toxic in themselves. For instance, nitrates in the water can poison infants through being converted into nitrites in their as yet incompletely developed systems. The nitrite becomes highly toxic when it combines with the blood haemoglobin.

In slower moving streams and lakes the effects of these substances may be serious. They act as fertilisers for algae and plant life. In consequence the area may become turbid and further oxygen depletion may take place as these organisms die and decay. This blooming of algae need not be serious if there are sufficient animals to eat them, but as always it is a question of degree. In some of the Great Lakes it is clear that the quantity of effluents added to the water has been much too high and a decline in water quality has followed.

The analysis and understanding of the effects of the multiplicity of chemicals of a more complex kind that now find their ways into rivers from sewage, the land or even the rain is often extremely difficult. From the point of view of pollution it is

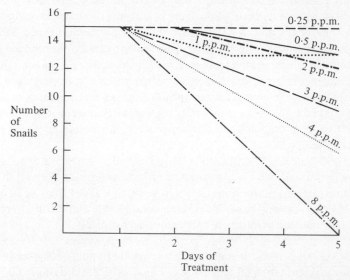

Fig. 5. Effect of domestic detergent on the survival of Jenkins' Spire Snail

often difficult to realise that a poison is reaching the water until some evidence of death or debilitation of the fish population occurs. It is often a long and tedious business to find out what the poison is, trace its source and prove its effect; in the meantime the biological community of the river may have been ruined.

Detergents are one example of a chemical effluent, the effects of which are better understood. Detergents may have direct biochemical effects on fish, for example trout are sensitive to detergents at only 1 part per million, but more often detergents affect them indirectly by lowering the concentration of oxygen in the water. Invertebrate organisms also are often killed by detergents, some of these being even more sensitive than fish. Figure 5 illustrates a simple laboratory experiment in which the effect of commercial washing-up liquid on the Jenkins' Spire Snail (*Hydrobia jenkinsi*) was investigated. Groups of snails were put in tanks in which different amounts of detergent had been added to the water. As can be seen from the diagram, even detergent at 0·5 part per million had a bad effect on the snails, and at 8 p.p.m. no snail was able to survive more than 5 days. A level of detergent as low as 0·1 part per million greatly reduces the rate at which oxygen is able to dissolve in the water. Modern detergents, such as sodium alkane sulphonate, foam less than earlier brands and this reduces the problem at sewage works where foaming could prevent efficient oxidation of the effluent. However, detergents, because of their immense domestic and industrial use, remain a serious hazard to many of our areas of fresh water.

Accidents involving the release of chemical substances into rivers and lakes are a very real problem, as the recent pollution of the Rhine has shown. Even quite small traces of many poisons can have unexpected effects; this is because fish 'process' a large quantity of water over their gill surfaces in carrying out gaseous exchange and in doing so a trace of the poison is inevitably absorbed and accumulated. In addition, fish and larger animals higher up the food chain will effectively concentrate the more persistent chemicals at each trophic or feeding level. Road tankers, railway wagons and barges containing any suspect chemical must be protected most carefully; too frequently the men in charge are not aware of the potential hazards of what they are carrying nor know the best procedure in the event of accident. Improved design of tankers with double skins and more effective legislation would go a long way towards putting this right.

Industrial and agricultural wastes still all too frequently enter our rivers and many of these have harmful effects on communities of lakes and rivers. With fresh water becoming an increasingly scarce commodity, it must be realised that the expense of cleaning-up water to make it palatable is often considerable and it is in every way preferable to prevent the pollution occurring in the first place.

POLLUTION OF THE SEA   It might seem impossible to pollute the sea but the almost weekly incidents with oil tankers have highlighted the situation and made us realise that the oceans are not as vast as we used to think. In fact pollution by oil released accidentally or in the undesirable activity of tank-cleaning is perhaps not as serious as many forms of marine pollution. Admittedly the coast and beaches may be fouled but biological degradation by yeast-like fungi and bacteria as well as some simple evaporation of the lighter fractions will eventually result in the total disappearance of the oil. Treating of the contaminated areas with emulsifiers (mostly detergents) does not break down the oil; it simply moves it on in small droplet form. Some of these emulsifiers are known to be extremely toxic to living things and in addition have a long life on the sea shore and in the sand. Other techniques being investigated include the use of mechanical booms and of a shredded polyurethane foam which has strong oil rather than water imbibing qualities (see Figs 6 and 7). Even so, large oil slicks occur too often and do great damage to seabirds. Even if these are picked up and cleaned, they have usually ingested so much oil in preening their oiled feathers that they are unable to feed and soon die, largely of starvation.

Fig. 6. A boom for enclosing an oil spillage

Fig. 7. A launch used for spraying dispersant on to an oil spillage

Where currents are insufficient to effect a proper mixing, some seas are also becoming polluted in the same way as fresh water. This may occur in estuaries, where raw effluents are often received, but there are recent reports of larger areas of water, such as the Baltic Sea, showing a marked biological deterioration in some parts.

POLLUTION OF THE LAND   Pollution of the land is perhaps less obvious than either air or water pollution but is nevertheless just as important. Rain may bring down a variety of contaminants such as traces of radioactive fall-out, fluoride and

11

sulphate ions. Since the ban on atmospheric nuclear tests, the first has become much less of a problem, but fluoride and sulphate could produce serious consequences. Fluoride is often released as a waste from industrial concerns such as aluminium works, and excess uptake may result in diseased bones and teeth, particularly in grazing farm animals such as sheep. Sulphate ions are important as more and more boiler systems are being converted to oil fuel which often has a high sulphur content. However, efforts are being made to reduce sulphur in the fuel oil and the main source of soil and land pollution is probably the farmer himself. He has a great variety of agricultural chemicals available and indeed much of the success of British post-war agriculture is a result of the use of such chemicals. These are broadly of three types: fertilisers, herbicides and pesticides. All of these can cause pollution in some form or another. Excess fertiliser will run-off into rivers; herbicides and pesticides may damage other organisms than those for which they are intended. There is some evidence that some of the brushwood-killers and defoliants which have been extensively used in forestry and warfare, may cause deformities and damage to animals. Field herbicides are all too often sprayed under even moderately windy conditions and the effect of the 'drift' of the spray is frequently disastrous for neighbouring woodland. Luckily the practice of road-verge spraying is now being reduced, but many attractive hedgerow flowers have disappeared. Pesticides remain a great problem. The organo-chlorine insecticides such as D.D.T. are still popular in many parts for the very reason that makes them unpopular in conservation — their persistence. In this way repeated spraying of a field, say of brussels sprouts against greenfly, is rendered unnecessary. At the present time alternative sprays such as the organo-phosphorus are still rather expensive and relatively dangerous to use but have little residual activity. For these reasons the replacement of the D.D.T. group is only progressing slowly. Other sprays, for instance fungicides, which may contain copper or tin, may also be potential hazards if they accumulate in the soil or run off into streams. However, provided the less desirable techniques such as seed treatment are avoided and care and good sense are used in the application of the less-persistent pesticides, it is possible that these substances now represent a less serious hazard and that the serious effects on bird life that occurred in the fifties and sixties will not be repeated. By way of example, a recent examination of a chalk stream trout which had wasted and died, possibly as a result of poisoning, came out as follows: hexachlorocyclohexane, 8 parts per 1000 million; D.D.E. (a breakdown compound of D.D.T.), 12 parts per 1000 million.

These concentrations are about one tenthousandth of the lethal dose. A dying trout maybe, but still perfectly edible! This occurred in an area where moderate use of pesticides on crops has gone on and where little direct run-off from the fields takes place. It could well be that the figure would be higher in other parts of the country.

Nevertheless, we ourselves may now be paying the penalty for the use of D.D.T. The average content of D.D.T. in man in Europe is probably about 7 parts per million, this being stored mainly in our fatty tissues, but breast-fed babies may face a special hazard as the concentration of the fat-soluble D.D.T. in milk (1968) may be 0·117 parts per million which is concentrated so as to add 0·017 mg D.D.T. per kg body weight per day; a level which is judged to be 70% above the maximum acceptable amount. There is still some doubt as to the physiological effects of D.D.T., but evidence is accumulating to show that it may have serious effects on the nervous system, and in consequence on animal behaviour.

A potentially serious agricultural hazard arises in intensive factory-type farming. Confining the animals in a limited area causes a problem of faeces disposal and farmers may be tempted to install a sewage plant, seemingly forgetting the value of old-fashioned farmyard manure. Liquid spillage from silage can also be dangerous if it finds its way into water; the high organic content will cause a serious depletion of oxygen. Both these two examples illustrate the point that, as a new technological method is developed, either in industry or in farming, the consequences and dangers inherent in the system must be anticipated and planned for. However, perhaps the dangers to the land do not lie so much in pollution as in the biologically dull monocultural fields, the result of an inevitably ruthless attempt to improve the economics of farming which often produce an environment more stultifying than a desert of sand. There is a danger that modern techniques may upset the soil environment in a long-term way so that its fertility may be impaired for future generations.

These problems of population, planning and pollution emphasise the urgency of a constructive conservation policy and it is the aim of this book to show how nature conservation operates both nationally and at a *personal* level.

2 The organisation of nature conservation in Britain

Inevitably it is often difficult for an individual, who happens to be interested in the Nature Conservation movement, to know what he or she can do in a practical way. The larger planning activities such as the South Hampshire plan, whilst constantly seeking information and advice at the local level, are seldom within the scope of the voluntary assistant. The most useful part a field natural historian can play is in helping the local nature conservation group, usually called the County Naturalists' Trust. There are a large number of conservation bodies operating in Britain and it may be worthwhile showing how their activities are related and interact with one another.

The history of nature conservation goes back to the foundation of the Royal Forests such as the New Forest and the Forest of Dean which were set up with the expressed intention of preserving the deer and later of producing timber. But the more natural history aspects of the conservation movement began with the foundation in 1889 of the Society for the Protection of Birds, later the Royal Society for the Protection of Birds (R.S.P.B.). By the turn of the century interest in plant and animal ecology was increasing and the concept of community types was coming to the fore. This led to the setting up of the Society for the Promotion of Nature Reserves (S.P.N.R.) in 1912, though it is only during the last few years that the co-ordinating role of this organisation has begun to help the various Naturalists' Trusts. 1926 saw the founding of the Council for the Protection of Rural England (C.P.R.E.) which has helped particularly by giving advice about footpaths, rights of way, the siting of buildings and tree preservation in beauty spots. Unfortunately perhaps its activities have been largely concerned with preserving things as they are, while the conservator accepts the necessity to modify the countryside, especially in relation to urban development.

The Nature Conservancy

A great step forward came in 1949 with the founding of the Nature Conservancy. This aimed to provide scientific advice on the conservation of the natural flora and fauna of Great Britain; to establish and manage nature reserves, including sites with physical features of scientific interest, and to develop scientific services such as research centres. Within the first ten years of its life the Nature Conservancy had established about 120 National Nature Reserves covering 1000 square kilometres. These reserves are scattered fairly evenly over the country and effectively cover most of the more important habitat types. The following tables give details of the main British habitat types and of the National Nature Reserves.

Table 4 The Major Habitats and Reserves in England, Wales and Scotland

The numbers indicate appropriate National Nature Reserves.
These are listed, by counties, in Table 5.

Habitat		England	Wales	Scotland
Maritime	1. Grassland	8, 23	75	117
	2. Salt marsh	51, 52		92
	3. Mudflat or sandy shore	39, 51, 52		
	4. Sand dune	7, 33, 34, 36, 39	60, 75, 76, 81, 83	87, 93, 99, 102, 117
	5. Shingle	34		
	6. Sea cliff	8	75	112, 114
	7. Estuary	39	74	
	8. Island	51, 52	86	95, 96, 97, 98, 108, 113, 115
Inland Grassland and Heath	1. Upland			
	(a) base rich	57		119
	(b) base poor	55	82	100, 110, 112
	2. Lowland			
	(a) chalk	1, 17, 27, 56		
	(b) limestone	8		
	(c) other			
	3. Lowland heath	14, 15, 38, 48, 49, 50, 54		
	4. Northern wet heath			
	5. Arctic alpine	57	62, 67, 68, 69, 85	88, 89, 101, 107, 109, 110, 117, 119
Fen and bog	1. Fen and Fen woodland (carr)	2, 3, 4, 6, 20, 21, 26, 29, 30, 35, 37	76	
	2. Raised bog	45	72	104
	3. Blanket bog	40	82	104, 118
	4. Southern valley bog	12, 46		
Fresh-water	1. Still			
	(a) base rich	5, 18		94, 99, 103
	(b) base poor			109, 116
	2. Running			
	3. Freshwater island			

Table 4—continued

	Habitat	England	Wales	Scotland
Woodland	1. Oak	9, 10, 11, 19, 41	61, 65, 66, 70, 71, 73, 77, 78, 79, 80, 84	
	2. Beech	42, 64		
	3. Ash	19, 43, 58, 59		111
	4. Birch	58	80	100, 101
	5. Alder	20, 21, 26, 29		
	6. Mixed deciduous	13, 16, 22, 25, 28, 32	63, 69	90, 109
	7. Pine	46		101, 110
	8. Juniper			91
	9. Yew	53		
	10. Mixed coniferous and deciduous	31		101
Other Habitats	1. Inland cliff		69, 70, 85	88, 89, 107, 119
	2. Gorge	57, 58	61, 71, 84	90, 111
Geological or physiographic		24, 47		

Table 5 The National Nature Reserves of England, Wales and Scotland

It should be noted that not all these areas are of free access; permits are often required. Full details are best obtained from the local office of the Nature Conservancy before visiting an area.

	County	Name	Grid reference	Acres	km^2	Description
ENGLAND						
1	Bedford	Knocking Hoe	TL 1132	22	0·09	Chalk down
2	Berks	Cothill	SU 4599	4	0·016	Fen
3	Cambridge	Wicken Fen	TL 5570	320	1·30	Fen
4	Cambridge	Chippenham Fen	TL 6469	193	0·78	Fen
5	Cheshire	Rostherne Mere	SJ 7484	327	1·32	Still water
6	Cheshire	Wybunbury Moss	SJ 6950	26	0·11	Floating bog
7	Devon	Braunton Burrows	SS 4437–4631	560	2·26	Dune
8	Devon	Axmouth – Lyme Regis Undercliffs	SY 2589–3391	793	3·20	Down and cliff
9	Devon	Bovey Valley Woodlands	SX 7582–8078	179	0·72	Oakwood

Table 5—continued

	County	Name	Grid reference	Acres	km²	Description

ENGLAND—continued

	County	Name	Grid reference	Acres	km²	Description
10	Devon	Yarner Wood	SX 7778	361	1·46	Oakwood
11	Devon	Dendles Wood	SX 6161	73	0·29	Oakwood
12	Dorset	Morden Bog	SY 9091	367	1·48	Bog
13	Dorset	Arne	SY 9586–9889	9	0·036	Wood
14	Dorset	Hartland Moor	SY 9485	214	0·86	Heath
15	Dorset	Studland Heath	SZ 0184	429	1·70	Heath
16	Essex	Hales Wood	TL 5740	20	0·08	Mixed wood
17	Hants	Old Winchester Hill	SU 6421	140	0·56	Downland
18	Herts	Tring Reservoirs	SP 9213–9012	49	0·20	Lake
19	Huntingdon and Peterborough	Castor Highlands	TF 1201	221	0·86	Oak and ash
20	Huntingdon and Peterborough	Holme Fen	TL 2288	640	2·56	Fen
21	Huntingdon and Peterborough	Woodwalton Fen	TL 2284	514	2·08	Fen
22	Huntingdon and Peterborough	Monks Wood	TL 1879–1980	387	1·56	Mixed wood
23	Kent	Northward Hill, High Halstow	TQ 7876	131	0·53	Coastal
24	Kent	Swanscombe Skull site	TQ 6174	5	0·02	Fossil man
25	Kent	Blean Woods	TR 1664–1864	165	0·66	Wood
26	Kent	Stodmarsh	TR 2261	300	1·21	Marsh
27	Kent	Wye and Crundale Downs	TR 0745	123	0·50	Chalk grassland
28	Kent	Ham Street Woods	TR 0033–0034	240	0·96	Wood
29	Lancs	Blelham Bog	NY 3700	5	0·02	Bog
30	Lancs	Esthwaite North Fen	SD 3597	4	0·016	Woodland and bog
31	Lancs	Rusland Moss	SD 3382	58	0·23	Wood and bog
32	Lancs	Roudsea Wood	SD 3382	287	1·16	Mixed wood
33	Lancs	Ainsdale Sand Dunes	SD 2912	1216	4·90	Dunes
34	Norfolk	Scolt Head Island	TF 8046	1821	7·36	Shingle and dune
35	Norfolk	Hickling Broad	TG 4122	1215	4·90	Fen
36	Norfolk	Winterton Dunes	TG 4920	259	1·02	Dunes
37	Norfolk	Bure Marshes	TG 3216–3515	1019	4·16	Marsh
38	Norfolk	Weeting Heath	TL 7888	338	1·36	Heath

Table 5—continued

	County	Name	Grid reference	Acres	km²	Description
ENGLAND—continued						
39	Northumber-land	Lindisfarne	NU 0447–1435	7378	29·6	Dunes, estuary sands and mudflats
40	Northumber-land	Coom Rigg Moss	NY 6979	88	0·35	Blanket bog
41	Oxford	Wychwood	SP 3316	647	2·60	Oakwood
42	Oxford	Aston Rowant	SU 7699–7497	166	0·65	Beechwood
43	Somerset	Rodney Stoke	ST 4849	86	0·35	Ashwood
44	Somerset	Bridgwater Bay	ST 2246–2959	6076	24·5	Coast
45	Somerset	Shapwick Heath	ST 4240	546	2·20	Raised bog
46	Stafford	Chartley Moss	SK 0029	104	0·42	Bog
47	Staffs and Worcester	Wren's Nest	SO 9392–9391	74	0·30	Limestone fossils
48	Suffolk	Thetford Heath	TL 8579	243	0·96	Heath
49	Suffolk	Cavenham Heath	TL 7672	337	1·36	Heath
50	Suffolk	Westleton Heath	TM 4667	117	0·46	Heath
51	Suffolk	Orfordness	TM 4549	249	0·97	Coast
52	Suffolk	Havergate	TM 4147	265	1·06	Coast
53	Sussex	Kingley Vale	SU 8210	230	0·93	Yewwood
54	Sussex	Lullington Heath	TQ 5302	155	0·63	Heath
55	Westmor-land	Moor House	NY 7729	10000	40·47	Moor
56	Wilts	Fyfield Down	SU 1470	612	2·46	Chalk downland
57	Yorks	Upper Teesdale	NY 8429–8024	6500	26·2	Arctic alpine, woodland, gorge
58	Yorks	Ling Gill	SD 7978	12	0·048	Limestone gorge, ash, birch
59	Yorks	Colt Park Wood	SD 7777	21	0·085	Ashwood
WALES						
60	Anglesey	Newborough Warren	SH 4165–3862	1566	6·32	Dune
61	Brecknock	Nant Irfon	SN 8355–8452	216	0·87	Oak and moor, gorge
62	Brecknock	Craig Cerrig Gleisind	SN 9420–9621	698	2·82	Mountain
63	Brecknock	Craig y Cilau	SO 1915	157	0·63	Wood with whitebeam
64	Brecknock	Cwm Clydach	SO 2012–2212	50	0·20	Beech in gorge
65	Caernarvon	Coed Gorswen	SH 7571	33	0·13	Oakwood
66	Caernarvon	Coed Dolgarrog	SH 7667	170	0·68	Oakwood

Table 5—continued

	County	Name	Grid reference	Acres	km²	Description
WALES—continued						
67	Caernarvon	Cwm Glas, Crafnant	SH 7360	38	0·15	Arctic alpine
68	Caernarvon	Cwm Idwal	SH 6559	984	4·0	Arctic alpine
69	Caernarvon	Snowdon	SH 6054–6452–6149	2300	9·24	Arctic alpine and woodland
70	Caernarvon	Coed Tremadoc	SH 5841	49	0·19	Oakwood and cliffs
71	Cardigan	Coed Rheidol (Devil's Bridge)	SN 7177	107	0·43	Oakwood and gorge
72	Cardigan	Cors Tregaron	SN 6863	1898	7·65	Raised bog
73	Carmarthen	Allt Rhyd y Groes	SN 7449–7747	153	0·62	Oakwood
74	Glamorgan	Whiteford (Burry Estuary)	SS 4496–4394	344	1·38	Estuary
75	Glamorgan	Gower Coast	SS 3887–4087	116	0·47	Coast
76	Glamorgan	Oxwich	SS 5087	542	2·20	Dune and fen
77	Merioneth	Coed Cymeran	SH 6842	65	0·26	Oakwood
78	Merioneth	Coeddyd Maentwrog	SH 6640	194	0·78	Oakwood
79	Merioneth	Coed Camlyn	SH 6539	57	0·23	Oakwood
80	Merioneth	Coed y Rhygen	SH 6836	52	0·21	Birch and oakwood
81	Merioneth	Morfa Harlech	SH 5535–5633	1214	5·0	Dune
82	Merioneth	Rhinog	SH 6530–6727	991	4·0	Moor and bog
83	Merioneth	Morfa Dyffryn	SH 5525–5623	500	2·0	Dune
84	Merioneth	Coed Ganllwyd (Blackfalls)	SH 7224	59	0·24	Oakwood and gorge
85	Merioneth	Cader Idris	SH 7113	969	3·9	Arctic alpine
86	Pembroke	Skomer	SM 7209	759	3·05	Island
SCOTLAND						
87	Aberdeen	Sands of Forvie	NK 0229–0024	1774	7·15	Dune
88	Aberdeen etc.	Caenlochan	NO 2079	8991	36·2	Arctic alpine and cliffs
89	Argyll and Perth	Ben Lui	NN 2627–2725	925	3·74	Arctic alpine
90	Bute	Glen Diomhan, Arran	NR 9346	24	0·096	Gorge
91	Dumfries	Tyron Juniper Wood	NX 8293	12	0·048	Juniper wood
92	Dumfries	Caerlaverock	NY 0066–0866	13514	55·0	Saltmarsh
93	Fife	Tentsmuir Point	NO 4928–5326	1249	5·03	Coastal and sand dune

Table 5—continued

	County	Name	Grid reference	Acres	km²	Description

SCOTLAND—continued

	County	Name	Grid reference	Acres	km²	Description
94	Fife	Morton Lochs	NO 4626	59	0·24	Lake
95	Fife	Isle of May	NT 6599	140	0·56	Island
96	Inner Isles	Rhum	NM 3698	26400	106	Island
97	Outer Isles	St. Kilda	NA 1506	2107	8·5	Island
98	Outer Isles	Monarch Islands	NF 6321			Island
99	Outer Isles	Loch Druidibeg, S. Uist	NF 7540–8037	4145	16·7	Loch and dune
100	Inverness	Craigellachie	NH 8812	642	2·60	Birchwood and moor
101	Inverness and Aberdeen	Cairngorms	NH 9208	58822	236	Pinewood and arctic alpine
102	Kincardine-Angus	St. Cyrus	NO 7564–7362	227	0·92	Shore and dune
103	Kinross	Loch Leven	NO 1401	3946	16·0	Loch
104	Kirkcudbright	Silver Flowe	NX 4684–4781	472	1·90	Blanket and raised bog
105	Kirkcudbright	Kirconnell Flow	NX 9769	383	1·56	Bog and pinewood
106	Perth	Rannock Moor	NN 4056–4252	3704	15·0	Bog
107	Perth	Meall nan Tarmachan (near Ben Lawers)	NN 5839–5637	1142	4·6	Arctic alpine
108	Ross and Cromarty (Outer Isles)	North Rona & Sula Sgeir	HW 8132, 6130	320	1·29	Island
109	Ross and Cromarty	Inverpolly	NC 0519	26827	108	Arctic alpine, woodland, lake
110	Ross and Cromarty	Beinn Eighe	NG 9767	10507	42·5	Pinewood and arctic alpine
111	Ross and Cromarty	Rassal Ashwood	NG 8443	202	0·81	Ashwood and gorge
112	Shetland	Hermaness, Unst	HP 6120–5912	2383	9·6	Coast, moor
113	Shetland	Haaf Gruney	HU 6398	44	0·17	Island
114	Shetland	Ronas Hill	HU 3083	7000	28·2	Cliffs, shore
115	Shetland	Noss	HU 5340	774	3·12	Island
116	Stirling-Dunbarton	Loch Lomond	NS 4190–3988 and 4487	624	2·50	Lake
117	Sutherland	Invernaver	NC 6762–7059	363	1·46	Beach and hills
118	Sutherland	Strathy Bog	NC 7953	120	0·48	Blanket bog
119	Sutherland	Inchnadamph	NC 2521	3200	13·0	Cliffs and grassland

At the same time the Nature Conservancy also set about the task of recording a large number of Sites of Special Scientific Interest (S.S.S.I.). Often these areas were quite small and usually unsuitable as major reserves, but it was felt desirable that they should be listed and the owners and County Councils informed. In this way misguided land use methods and planning could be avoided. Whilst it is perhaps doubtful if a scheduled S.S.S.I. has often deterred anyone from carrying out a development, it is possible that the recognition of the sites following their recent and more detailed study may be of more use in the future. The Conservancy activities of research and advising have improved greatly as experience has been gained; and one of their main functions outside the managing of nature reserves must be in advising the planners and in helping local groups organise the management of their reserves.

The National Parks

To some there is one aspect of National Conservation planning that must seem a little disappointing; this is the formation of National Parks. These were first mooted in the 1940's but were mostly set up in the early 'fifties and, along with green belts and other broader aspects of national planning, have not always proved a fully workable proposition. To many of us the National Park concept is modelled on thoughts of the great African and American parks where the public are frequently only admitted after paying a fee and few people are allowed to live in the area. Parts of the park may be allocated for recreation and other parts designated sanctuary areas. In some areas in many American National Parks, no cars, houses or dogs are allowed; you visit the area on horseback or on foot and you carry in your food and equipment.

These superb parks are, regrettably, an almost impossible ideal in this country where the most suitable areas are often already quite densely populated both by permanent residents earning their livelihood and also by the vast numbers of holiday visitors. The list (Table 6) of the ten National Parks in England and Wales includes many of our most famous holiday areas and 'beauty-spots'. Here conservation must encourage visitors to make the best use of the area without spoiling it, while the residents and planners must try to see that accommodation, roads, car parks, restaurants, lavatories and other facilities are provided with minimum interference to the amenity value of the area. The term 'beauty-spot' itself is too often equated with litter, cars and kiosks and many would wish that control in our National Parks should be more strictly observed both at the planning and at the wardening levels.

There are no National Parks in Scotland; this is at least partly due to the relatively lighter pressure on many of the outstanding areas and also because many are already National Nature Reserves (e.g. the Cairngorms, see p. 35). However, new roads are

Table 6 National Parks of England and Wales

Area	Extent km^2	Habitats and Interest	Recreation
Brecon Beacons	1340	Moor and mountain	Climbing, walking, fishing
Dartmoor	950	Moor, wooded valleys, 'tors'	Riding, walking, fishing
Exmoor	690	Moor, wooded valleys, ponies, red deer	Riding, walking, fishing
Lake District	2240	Lakes, mountains, dales, woods, rivers	Climbing, walking, sailing, camping etc.
Northumberland	1030	River valleys, moors, Pennine way, Hadrian's wall	Walking, riding, fishing
North Yorkshire Moors	1440	Cliffs, moors, peaks or 'toppings', forest, architecture	Sailing, walking, fishing
Peak District	1400	Limestone hills, Kinder Scout (652 m) river valleys, caves	Walking, pot-holing, fishing
Pembrokeshire Coast	440	Cliffs, beaches, grassland	Walking (coast path), bathing, sailing, archaeology
Snowdonia	2200	Mountain, rock, scree and alpine grassland, rivers and lakes	Walking, climbing, fishing, archaeology
Yorkshire Dales	1760	Limestone hills, moorland, woodland, gorges	Walking, climbing, riding, fishing, pot-holing

being opened in the North West and it would seem to be only a matter of time before control such as occurs in our English National Parks must be exercised.

The National Trust and the Forestry Commission

Two other national organisations have had a profound effect on conservation in Britain; these are the National Trust and the Forestry Commission. The former, founded in 1895 with the intention of preserving places of historic interest or natural beauty, has not been particularly active in the more deliberate conservation of nature but, by acquiring land and fostering public interest, has provided a magnificent service to the country. Recently it has taken up a more active conservation attitude, particularly by leasing its reserves for management by local enthusiasts. The Forestry Commission is also now more aware of its responsibilities and has set up a number of Forest Reserves and National Forest Parks organised Nature Trails and generally seems to be allowing more public access to its forests than formerly.

County Open Spaces

There are a number of other national societies and trusts which have set up reserves, many of these being concerned with wildfowl, but during the last few years conservation has come much more within the scope of county planning. Countryside committees, taking advice from many clubs and societies concerned with conservation, amenity and use of the country, have been set up and Public Open Spaces acquired. In Hampshire, for instance, there are about twenty-four of these, ranging from little more than a car park with a good view to an area of a few square kilometres which could be called a County Park. In these areas the emphasis is often most strongly on amenity and recreation but many sites are also useful for natural history activities and some are large enough to include proper nature reserves (e.g. see Fig. 2 on p. 4 and the account of Crab Wood on p. 54). Within these reserves it may be possible to designate some special sites as sanctuaries where public access is restricted.

County Naturalists' Trusts

The County Council will most often draw assistance from the local County Naturalists' Trust for the management of these Public Open-Space Nature Reserves and the County is able to help with funds, manpower, wardens and capital equipment. The Naturalists' Trust themselves usually own or rent a number of Local Nature Reserves (L.N.R.s) and it is towards these that much of the local natural history interest will be directed. The strength of a Naturalists' Trust lies in its local knowledge, not only of communities and rarities but of long-term trends. Even if these are subjective or speculative, they may be a valuable addition to a management plan. A Trust may run a variety of reserves with different aims in mind. It may want to possess one example of each major habitat within the county; it may be desirable to protect a rare or local species; or the reserve may be for use in education and possibly managed by a school.

Apart from financial problems, which are so serious that few Trusts are able to buy large areas of land, the main problem that they still have to face is recruiting active people who are prepared to survey and manage reserves. What is needed is a blend of the local natural history society with that of the more active conservation corps. The chapters that follow are designed to show how something of this kind may be achieved.

3 The management of reserves

The problems

Conservation must by its very nature be a practical science and yet so often the various management activities involved might be regarded more as an art than a science. This is due to a number of causes. First, the uniqueness of almost any area being worked on makes it difficult to extrapolate from previous experience, and second, there is often a degree of urgency in the work that makes proper scientific preliminary work, such as detailed survey, difficult.

Indeed some conservation activities differ little from what has been called 'wild gardening', but I do not think this should be regarded as an implied criticism. Horticulture itself relies on acquired expertise and considerable scientific backing as well as aesthetic aims. The successful management of Nature Reserves depends on similar background. The only problems perhaps are the scale of the operation in time and space and the lack of a heritage of experience. In some ways these problems all serve to make practical conservation a more interesting and even exciting activity.

Survey

Selection of a reserve and its management must depend on some sort of preliminary survey. As work on the reserve progresses more detailed surveys will be carried out from year to year, which may result in the management policies being modified.

The preliminary survey is inevitably rather qualitative, but the following notes could act as a guide which could do little more than establish whether the area is workable as a reserve at all. Much of this information should have been collected after only a few visits to the site (see Table 7).

There is a lot to be said for having a more or less standard survey procedure at all levels. In the case of the preliminary survey it may turn out that the site is unsatisfactory as a reserve at the time, but circumstances may change and filing and reference will be easier if a standardised procedure is adopted.

Listing and recording of species in preliminary and later surveys gives point to more conventional natural history activities, particularly of local groups. However, it is desirable to have much more detailed, quantitative data if the success of the various management policies is to be realised. Here the emphasis shifts, as we may be concerned with the balance of the community, with the size and distribution of the dominant trees, the amount of bare ground and the balance of living things within the area.

Table 7

Notes on the carrying out of a preliminary survey of a reserve

1. *Name of the area.*   2. *Type of habitat.*
3. *Location* (Grid reference).   4. *Extent.*
5. *Relation to surrounding countryside* (This could be of particular importance in small areas where disturbance might ruin the area unless animals have a chance to move to neighbouring land).
6. *Sketch map of the area* showing sub-habitats and areas of special interest.
7. Notes on footpaths, rights of way, existing land use and other 'outside' factors.
8. *Species lists* probably best recorded initially on Biological Records Centre cards,* but a note as to the abundance of species is worthwhile.
9. *Species of special interest* including a note as to their exact location, abundance and any immediate conservation needs.
10. *Management.* Any preliminary suggestions.

AERIAL SURVEYS   Although rather expensive, aerial photography provides one of the quickest and simplest ways of obtaining a general record of an area. Figure 8 shows a view of a County Open Space, Danebury Hill in Hampshire, taken in 1924.

Figure 9 shows the same area taken in 1968; it is interesting to note the only moderate increase in the growth of hawthorn scrub (A). Aerial surveys must of course be backed up by detailed work on the ground. The 1924 view also shows some areas from which the turf had been cut (B). These areas are now the most interesting and varied botanically, but this is only shown from work on the ground.

TRANSECTS   A relatively quick way of carrying out a ground survey is to make a series of transects or vertical sections, say 25 m. apart, from marked posts, working across the area. In a wood, for instance, the data may be recorded graphically, with a pictorial note of the species, size and quality of the timber (see Fig. 30 on page 59), and also with photographs. If this is too complicated, simpler species lists may be made. While these techniques are more suitable for recording plants, birds may be recorded similarly or perhaps more effectively by walking a well-defined path and noting all the birds seen in a given time (see also page 48). Knowledge of bird song and behaviour can also be used to provide a guide to the numbers of nesting birds in the area.

QUADRATS   A quadrat can conveniently consist of a wooden or metal frame, one metre square, with wires stretched across it at every hundred millimetres. It is

* Available from the Nature Conservancy Biological Records Centre, Monks Wood, Huntingdon.

Fig. 8. Danebury Hill near Stockbridge, Hampshire. Summer view in 1924

Fig. 9. Danebury Hill. Winter view in 1968. Note moderate increase in the growth of hawthorn (A) and recolonisation of de-turfed area (B)

primarily used for recording the ground flora and is particularly useful for continuous year by year recording. The data may be recorded graphically or photographically. Unfortunately, quadrats take a great deal of time to record and, while it is much more useful to take several samples, perhaps at random over the area, a small number of accurately fixed quadrats, marked with reference and sunken pegs, can be extremely useful.

A case in point arose at the County Open Space at Abbotstone Down, near Alresford in Hampshire where intense public use was having a detrimental effect on

Table 8 Abbotstone Down, near Alresford, Hampshire

Analysis of the plants in two 1 m^2 Quadrats

Quadrat A		Date		
Area receiving intense wear from cars and walkers		1967	1968	1969
	Number of species of flowering plants and mosses	21	25	20
	Bare ground %	14·3	9·2	10·6
	Ground covered by white clover (*Trifolium repens*) %	2·1	18·1	20·2
Quadrat B	Number of species of flowering plants and mosses	24	22	17
Area adjacent to A but receiving little or no wear	Bare ground %	0	0	0

the quality of the grassland. A week-end survey of the area was carried out in mid-June over three years. The data obtained from the quadrats (Fig. 10) shows that, on the worn site (quadrat A), the total species list declined only slightly and the area of bare ground became smaller, but that this was offset by the growth of white clover.

During this period some effort was made to control the access of vehicles and this could have been partly responsible for the probable improvement. However, it is particularly interesting to compare the data in quadrat A with that of the 'control', unworn site, quadrat B. During the same period, although there was no bare ground and little growth of clover, the area showed a marked decline in species, particularly

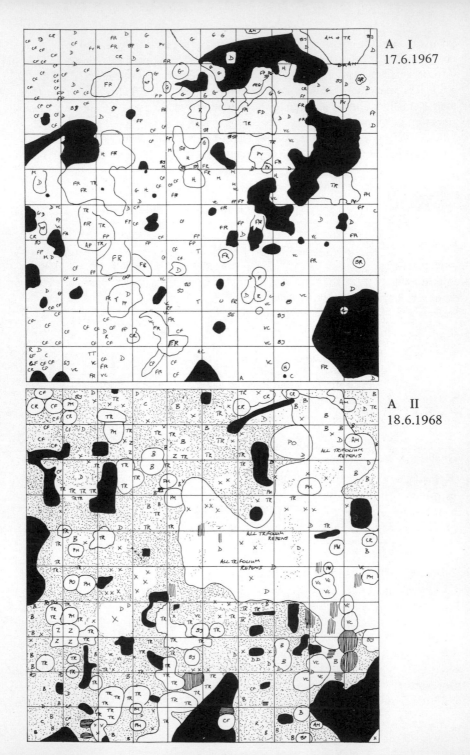

A I
17.6.1967

A II
18.6.1968

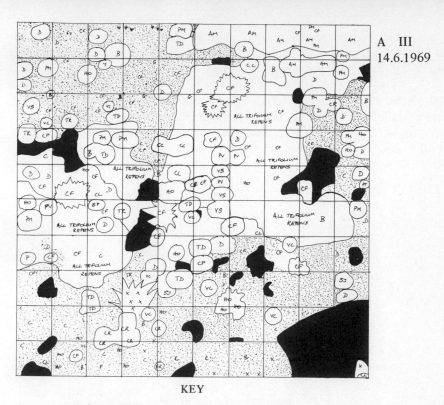

KEY

AM	*Achillea millifolia*	H	*Hypochaeris radicata*
Y	*Asperula cynanchica*	‖‖‖	*Lolium perenne*
≡	*Barbula* (moss)	PM	*Plantago major*
	Bare ground	P	*Plantago media*
B	*Bellis perennis*	PO	*Poa annua*
CR	*Campanula rotundifolia*	PV	*Polygala vulgaris*
⚹	*Camptothecium* (moss)	PS	*Poterium sanguisorba*
CF	*Carex flacca*	PV	*Prunella vulgaris*
C	*Cerastium* sp.	R	*Ranunculus repens*
GL	*Cladonia* sp.	SP	*Sagina procumbens*
CC	*Crepis capillaris*	SJ	*Senecio jacobaea*
⸚	*Festuca ovina*	D	*Taraxacum laevigatum*
FR	*Festuca rubra*	T	*Thymus drucei*
FV	*Fragaria vesca*	TD	*Trifolium dubium*
G	*Galium saxatile*	TR	*Trifolium repens*
HO	*Holcus lanatus*	X/Z	*Trisetum flavescens*
MP	*Hypnum cupressiforme* (moss)	VC	*Veronica chamaedrys*

Fig. 10. Abbotstone Down quadrats. 1 m² quadrats taken in successive years at exactly the same site on worn grass by a picnic table.

the more attractive ones such as common rockrose (*Helianthemum chamaecistus*). This suggests that environmental conditions, other than those induced by man, may in this instance have had a profound effect on the flora.

SURVEYING THE ANIMAL POPULATIONS   Inevitably survey of the animals is more difficult than the plants. Some suggestions for surveying the bird population, other than by netting and trapping have already been mentioned. If the area is extensive, mist-netting may be warranted; but too often the information gained by netting and ringing is of little value for the general survey of the area and the disturbance may not be beneficial to the reserve. However, there is no doubt that

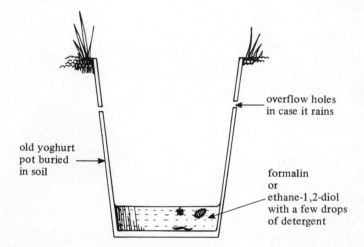

overflow holes
in case it rains

old yoghurt
pot buried
in soil

formalin
or
ethane-1,2-diol
with a few drops
of detergent

Fig. 11. Pitfall trap for collecting small invertebrates

useful work, perhaps on one species, may be done where there is a specific aim in mind. For instance it may be desirable to know the exact density of Blue Tits in an area before putting up nest boxes, so that a comparison may be made afterwards. If ringing is to be carried out, it is necessary to obtain a permit from the British Trust for Ornithology first. Further details of the various trapping and ringing procedures are given in Dowdeswell's *Practical Animal Ecology*, Chapter 3.

Butterflies have always been popular Natural History material and their survey by constant collecting (and release) is an essential part of long-term survey. Moths may be sampled, perhaps more quantitatively, using a portable mercury-vapour moth trap, but the sampling of both these groups is notoriously subject to temporary climatic changes and many samples must be taken before they can be relied upon in any quantitative sense.

The smaller invertebrate animals are often neglected in survey work and these are particularly suited to study in schools. A simple sampling technique involves the use of pitfall traps (see Fig. 11). Small polystyrene pots are buried in the turf or ground and any small animal that falls in is killed in a solution of formalin or ethane-1,2-diol at the bottom. Small overflow holes should be arranged in case a rainstorm occurs. Results of a survey using a large number of traps on three separate Dorset localities (which are all National Nature Reserves) are illustrated in Fig. 12. These results indicate the peak of male activity of the hunting spider *Lycosa tarsalis* in May, while that of the female is in August. The differing distribution of the spider

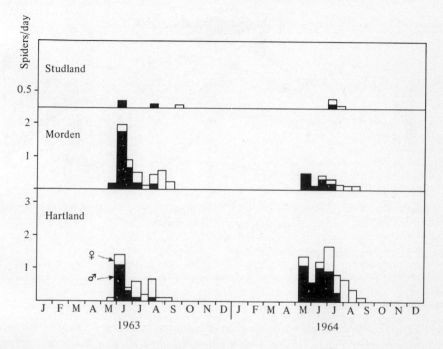

Fig. 12. Activity of the hunting spider Lycosa tarsalis *on Dorset heaths (from* The Phrenology of Spiders on Heathland in Dorset *by P. Merrett, J. Zool., London (1968) 156, pp 239-256)*

in the three areas is also emphasised. This work can be repeated year by year and changes in the invertebrate population assessed.

Mammals are perhaps the most overlooked of all. The simplest way to survey the larger mammals is by keeping quiet and watching for them. Sometimes the use of a hide comes into its own here, particularly if the hide is sited on stilts overlooking a popular feeding or watering place. Small mammals are best sampled by trapping, using a live-catching trap such as the Longworth trap (Fig. 13). The results of such a survey are discussed on page 53.

Whatever the survey technique, it is in long-term recording of these sorts that School and other Natural History organisations can be of great value. It is alarming to note how little useful quantitative data we have about our areas from more than ten years ago.

TUNNEL   NEST BOX

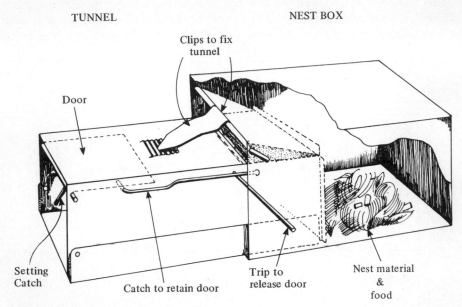

Fig. 13. Longworth small mammal trap

Management policies

As a general policy any plan is better than no plan but it is no good expecting the first management plan to be in any sense permanent and binding. By its very nature conservation must involve modification of ideas and planning as experience is gained and environmental circumstances alter. Indeed it would be a shame if a rigid management plan stultified progress by necessitating continuous reappraisal at the committee level.

At the start it is essential to review the purposes for which the reserve was created. Are the main aims public recreation and amenity, is the area representative of a particular community or habitat, is it for the protection of rarities or is it for scientific or educational use? A reserve may involve all these aims, or the suitability for one of them such as amenity may outweigh the others, as it would for instance in an urban area.

Much of the management plan must be devoted to short and long-term management proposals. These will depend to a large extent on the existing land use pattern. Unless there is any good reason for changing the land use, for instance if a particular activity such as spraying is endangering the community, the general rule should be that the same policies be continued. A reserve does not mean that the area should necessarily 'go wild'. Usually the effect of leaving areas of grassland and even woodland alone is that they become dominated by uninteresting species such as bramble, nettle and hawthorn. There is an interesting philosophical point here: should nature be allowed to look after itself, even at the expense of the species which man finds particularly interesting?

'Dull' species will allow some wild life to prosper, but, if the aims of conservation in terms of amenity and maintenance of a variety of wildlife are to be achieved, such a laissez-faire policy does not usually work. However, whether or not there is an existing land-use policy which may help maintain the habitat, it is worthwhile pointing out that there are few areas in Britain where some sort of intensive land management has not been carried out for hundreds of years. These notes on the writing of a management plan, following on from the preliminary survey, may be a useful guide:

Table 9 Notes on the writing of a management plan

1. *Name of the area*	3. *Type of Habitat*
2. *Location* (Grid reference)	4. *Extent*

5. *General description of the area*, including a detailed map

6. *Reasons for the creation of the reserve*

    (a) Public recreation and amenity.
    (b) Importance as a community type.
    (c) Interesting and rare species.
    (d) Scientific value.
    (e) Educational use.

7. *Detailed description of the area*

(a) Topography	(e) Flora
(b) Geology	(f) Fauna
(c) Climate	(g) Land use
(d) Soils	(h) Archaeology
	(i) Other interests

8. *Tenure* Whether freehold, leasehold or held under an agreement with the owner. Length of any lease or agreement and amount of any rent.

9. *Land use* Arrangements regarding grazing, agriculture and forestry at present in force.

10. *Sporting rights* Shooting and fishing rights; who holds them and the degree to which they are exercised.

Table 9—continued

11. *Access arrangements* Public access and rights of way. Need for permit.

12. *Maintenance* Any liability for upkeep of fences, ditches, drains, tracks, paths, sea walls, embankments, buildings etc.

13. *Short-term management proposals*

    (a) *Adjustments to existing landuse activities*
    (b) *Path clearing*
    (c) *Pest and weed control*, e.g. clearance of scrub, nettles.
    (d) *Reserve equipment*, e.g. notice boards, nest boxes, hides, boats, vehicles, tools.
    (e) *Wardening* Need for paid or volunteer wardens.
    (f) *Any special problems*

14. *Long-term management proposals*

    (a) *Changes in land use*
    (b) *Planting plans*
    (c) *Construction of ponds, streams, drainage ditches*
    (d) *Car parks, information centre*

15. *Management responsibility* Names and addresses of the field team leader, the reserve committee, wardens and local interested bodies.

16. *Research* Details of scientific work proposed or being carried out.

17. *Progress* Priorities, time schedule, reports and revision of the management plan.

    Information and general enquiries should be sent to the field team leader.

A plan of this sort should ensure reasonable uniformity in the handling of the reserves in an area, and with a copy in the hands of the conservation officer of the local Naturalists' Trust, should avoid misunderstandings and inefficiency. The various management policies will be coordinated by a field team leader who lives near the reserve and is in touch with local organisations and enthusiasts. Initially the management plan must be approved by the conservation committee (or similar body) and no long-term changes in management policy should be carried out without the approval of such a committee. Apart from trivial expenditure on the reserve, all proposals involving more serious expenditure should first be submitted to the conservation committee. This should not involve the field team leader in too much paper-work and should make the efficient running of the reserve much easier.

The following three chapters deal with the detailed management of a National Park, Local Nature Reserves and Single Species Conservation Areas. Regardless of size and aims, in most cases the survey policies suggested above will have to be carried out if the successful management of the area is to be achieved.

4 National nature reserves

It would be ideal if we could have a series of really large nature reserves covering all the major habitats and communities throughout the country. Areas large enough to be 'biologically viable'; capable of sustaining change due to natural environmental changes and successions, to management policies and perhaps intensive public use. With the price of land rising continuously it is perhaps remarkable that the Nature Conservancy has been able to establish over 120 National Nature Reserves covering well over a thousand square kilometres throughout the country. Inevitably the reserves are small, perhaps too small and infrequent in the south, but certainly in the north country, where the use of land is less intensive, reserves of adequate size have been set up.

One of the best known of these is the Cairngorms National Nature Reserve (Figs 14 and 15), lying between the valleys of the Spey and Dee and comprising 240 km² of wild countryside and mountains. Many of the mountains are over 1300 metres high and some of the glens and lochs lie above 1000 metres. There are very fine woods of birch and natural pine at lower altitudes and the area abounds with interesting plants and animals and is close by the site where the Osprey (see page 71) has returned to breed. Even though the area appears so vast, some of the same problems of management exist here as in the smaller reserves of the south. These problems are caused mainly by the variety of human interests in the area.

Primarily perhaps, the area is of value as a tourist attraction; there is excellent skiing on the north slopes; there are many magnificent climbs and walks. These activities are sponsored and encouraged by the Cairngorms Winter Sports Development Board and the Scottish Council for Physical Recreation. In addition there are the interests of the commercial foresters, the Forestry Commission, and last but not least the local landowners. These may also exercise their sporting rights over parts of the area, and may shoot grouse, stalk deer and fish for trout. Some of these activities may be available to visitors if the necessary permission and permits are obtained. It has been the job of the Nature Conservancy, although they actually only own a small part of the reserve, to try to effect collaboration between these interests with a view to the long-term conservation of the area.

The woodlands are a particularly interesting and extensive relic of the original Caledonian Forest which must at one time have covered much of the lower slopes of the mountains with a varied pattern of trees of different ages, interspersed with more open glades — a community differing markedly from the close and seried ranks of a forestry plantation. Young pine trees have a high light requirement and regeneration seems to take place best in the more open clearings. In this way a more varied and patchy community is produced which supports a wider variety of plant

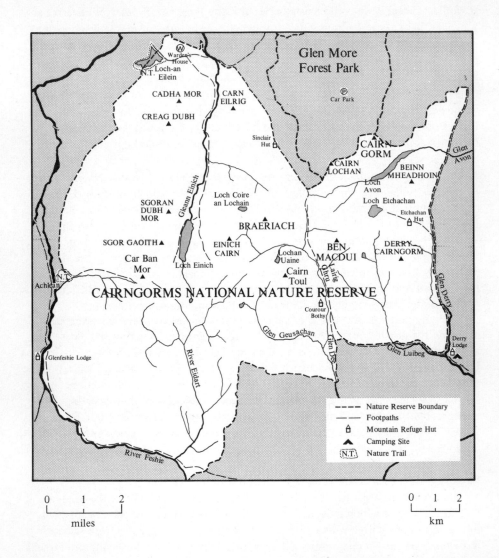

Fig. 14. Map of the Cairngorms (Modified from the Nature Conservancy guide)

Fig. 15. The Lairig Ghru in the Cairngorms National Nature Reserve, looking NNW from the Aberdeenshire side

and animal life. Efforts to re-establish pine-woods where they have been eliminated by grazing or fire should bear this regeneration pattern in mind.

There are many shrubs in these woods, principally bilberry (*Vaccinium myrtillus*), crowberry (*Empetrum hermaphroditum*) and ling (*Calluna vulgaris*), but the herbs are interesting and include two species of orchid, the creeping ladies tresses (*Goodyera repens*) and lesser twayblade (*Listera cordata*), as well as chickweed wintergreen (*Trientalis europaea*) and bitter vetch (*Vicia orobus*). The woodlands are also renowned for their interesting animals. Roe deer may be seen quite commonly as well as the red squirrel and much rarer pine marten.

Bird life in the woods is particularly noteworthy.* Crossbill, siskin and crested tit all breed in the more wooded parts of the reserve, as do the more unusual game birds: capercaillie and black grouse.

On the higher ground between 500 and 700 metres ericaceous plants such as ling and heathers replace the trees and at still higher altitudes the flora becomes more typically arctic-alpine with many interesting plants such as starwort mouse-ear chickweed (*Cerastium cerastioides*) and starry saxifrage (*Saxifraga stellaris*) in the damper and richer 'flushes' giving way to mountain crowberry (*Empetrum hermaphroditum*) and trailing azalea (*Loiseleuria procumbens*) on the drier and

* An excellent film 'Birds of Strathspey' is available from the Royal Society for the protection of Birds, The Lodge, Sandy, Bedfordshire.

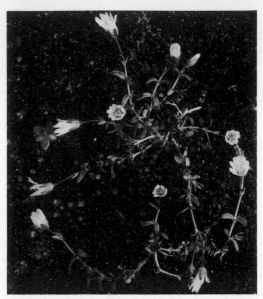

Fig. 16. An alpine plant, Starwort Mouse-ear Chickweed (Cerastium cerastioides), which is quite common in the Cairngorms

more exposed areas over 800 metres. The flora of the exposed ridges is particularly interesting and surprisingly varied; it includes plants adapted to some of the most rigorous conditions in the British Isles, with mosses, liverworts and lichens playing an important part in the community which is essentially a tundra ecosystem. The community is often called a *Rhacomitrium-heath*. The unstable nature of the soil, due to the effects of frost, wind and rain, results in frequent erosion and bare patches of detritus appear. These are usually colonised by lichens (*Cetrarias*) and mosses, particularly the woolly hair-moss (*Rhacomitrium lanuginosum*), the carpet of which may become colonised by sedges and sheep's fescue (*Festuca ovina*). Dwarf shrubs such as crowberry may act as 'anchor-plants' to the whole, the mosses developing in the more sheltered areas and in their turn providing a niche for young plants of the shrubs to develop (see Fig. 17).

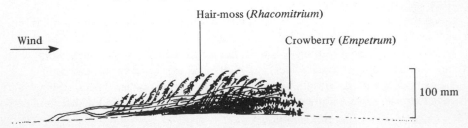

Fig. 17. Rhacomitrium heath above 1000 m

Although this community forms a patchy and diminutive cover over the mountain tops, it is still a complex one and, if upset by excessive wear due to walking, riding, skiing and grazing, could fail to maintain itself. The resulting increase in the size of the bare patches could promote erosion which would not only look unsightly but could have many untoward effects on the whole area.

These mountain tops are the haunts and breeding sites of the ptarmigan and dotterel, while on the lower hills greenshank are common. The heads of the corries are often lined with cliffs and screes; golden eagle and peregrine breed on these cliffs, while ring ouzel is quite often seen in the screes at the cliff foot.

The problem of management of an area of this size and importance is clearly considerable. Much of the basic survey work has been done with regard to the climate, soils, fauna and flora of the area, but such work, particularly of a quantitative nature, must go on. In the past the land use of the area has not always been all it might have been from the point of view of conservation. Excessive felling of the Scots pine has taken place, particularly because of needs in wartime, and the effects of deer browsing the young trees and of fires have also been serious. Considerable research has gone into trying to establish the best techniques for rehabilitating these woodlands; deer-proof fences have been set up to prevent deer-damage and allow for regeneration to take place; pine trees have been planted in areas where trees had been eradicated. However, as the lower areas of the reserve become recolonised, no doubt the management policies will have to be modified. The habit of burning the moor to allow for the development of young and healthy heather has been carried out for many years. This may suit the grouse and undoubtedly helps produce the colourful late-summer heather-moor that is one of the main attractions of the area, but it certainly has adverse effects on many of the other plant and animal inhabitants. The effects of grazing are more difficult to analyse. Some grazing by sheep or deer is necessary if the grass is to be kept cropped and of good quality. In a reserve like this it is probably best for red deer to be the main grazing animal of the uplands, as they will forage for food much higher than sheep. Fortunately or unfortunately, these deer have no predators other than man in Britain and as a result over-population can easily set in. Grass may be over-grazed and regenerating trees damaged. In difficult times the deer may invade neighbouring farmland and cause considerable damage. Accordingly it is vital that the optimum size of herd for the area should be worked out and shooting or culling arranged to remove old or poor animals and keep the herd at the right size. This will provide income for the various estates on the area by providing sport, employing stalkers and selling venison, antlers and skins.

Reindeer, which were last heard of in Scotland 800 years ago, have been introduced just outside the reserve, on the northern slopes of the Cairngorms. These feed mainly on lichens and should not compete with the deer. Domesticated Scandinavian stock was used for this introduction and by 1965 there were thirty head which had been raised in the area. By 1970 this number had risen to eighty-one.

This considerable increase has been achieved despite steady culling for sales of meat and skins, for research and for live sales to zoos. The animals seem to be settling down well and add considerable interest to the area, as well as contributing towards the economic use of the land. Nevertheless, as with all types of introduction their habits and herd size will have to be watched carefully in the years ahead. (See Fig. 18.)

The most serious problems relate to the ever increasing number of visitors to the area, a fact which, in itself, underlines the importance of the reserve in every way. As always, conservationists find themselves in a cleft-stick on this point. It is one of the aims of the conservation movement to encourage people to take a greater interest in their natural environment, yet what is the point if there is shortly to be no interesting nature left? The temptation might be to say that in a reserve of this

Fig. 18. A reindeer ox in the Cairngorms

size this is no serious worry; a disturbed species may simply move to a less disturbed site. Whilst this may be true, it is clearly a question of time and degree. Ever increasing numbers of visitors will cause more and more wear on the paths and hilltops and progressively more disturbance to the fauna.

This is where the visitors must be regarded as part of the reserve and managed too! Considerable subtlety is needed to do this as no one likes to be told to do something or more particularly not to do it. In the winter and spring many people come to the ski slopes which are mostly just outside the reserve in the Glen More Forest Park, where there is an information centre and restaurant, and so the disturbance factor within the reserve should be fairly low. In summertime the chair lift on the north side of Cairngorm will carry a large number of visitors into the reserve and this could be more serious. Luckily most people wish to keep to the paths and so nesting birds should not be disturbed. Dogs can be a problem and may have to be kept on a lead, while any public use regrettably results in litter. Camping and fires are not allowed except at three sites just outside the area so as to avoid any risk to the vegetation, but there are three emergency shelters in the reserve.

One way in which visitors to an area can be ducted through it most effectively is through the organisation of a marked route or Nature Trail. These have the advantage of keeping people moving in one direction only — infinitely preferable to continuously meeting visitors doing the circuit the other way round — as well as providing useful information as to what can be seen. It is also possible to organise a

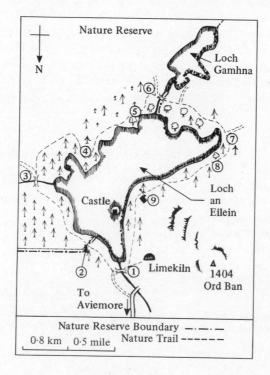

Fig. 19. Map of the Loch an Eilein Nature Trail

trail so that people are deliberately kept away from some rarity. There is no doubt that Nature Trails are enjoyed by children particularly, and in some areas it has been possible to write a trail specially for children, with simple questions, sketches and diagrams (which can be coloured), as well as trails for more adult visitors. Even the more experienced field naturalists usually confess to having learned a great deal from such trails.

There are two trails in the reserve, one at Loch an Eilein (Figs 19 and 20) and one at Achlean in Glen Feshie. Both of these are highly informative and include delightful sketches of squirrel, duck, deer and orchids, which form a ready aid to identification and will be valuable to old and young alike. The use of Nature Trails forms such a useful part of reserve management that it is worthwhile including a synopsis of the Loch an Eilein trail which may be a help in the writing and setting-up of trails even if they are not in such spectacular country. Before beginning the Trail, the Nature Conservancy guide giving details both of the area as a whole and of the various stands along the route should be obtained. It is on sale locally in hotels and shops.

The final note in this Nature Trail draws attention to the Reserve Wardens on whom so much of the success of a reserve depends. In all there are three Wardens for the whole 240 square kilometres of this National Nature Reserve. They must help visitors in countless ways; on Nature Trails, giving directions and generally being sources of information as well as acting as policemen in preventing abuses such as fires and the leaving of litter. Just as important is their responsibility to wildlife in helping to manage the flora and fauna of the Reserve.

Table 10 Synopsis of the Loch an Eilein Nature Trail Guide

A. *The Cairngorms Nature Reserve*
   A general account of the reserve as a whole, its size, ownership, topography, fauna and flora.

B. *Special Notices*
   Visitors are asked to: Avoid fire risk, keep to the paths, close gates, keep dogs under control, leave no litter.

C. *Distance* of the trail: 4 km
   Time to cover the nine points of the trail: about 2 hours.

D. *The Trail*
   Point 1   *The Old Lime Kiln.* Limestone quarry nearby – good view of birchwoods – buzzard often seen wheeling and soaring – crossbills often seen in larch by

   loch shore – view of loch and castle.
   Point 2   *Trail enters Nature Reserve.* Pine scales and cones – red squirrel activity –

Table 10—continued

Point 2—continued

dense pinewood — mosses — bilberry and blaeberry — good quality pine used as

a 'seed-tree' by the Forestry Commission.

Point 3   *Bridge.* Large boulders and the ice age — thieves road — effects of felling pines.

Point 4   *Water Lilies.* Wild duck, mergansers and whooper swans — trout and the effect of predatory pike — pine regeneration — pine resin gall moth — capercaillie.

Point 5   *Aspen Trees.* Birds on the loch — ospreys, sandpipers, goosanders and dippers — red-green tiger beetle — holly.

Point 6   *Loch Gamhna.* Former grazing of nearby land — reed beds and the silting up of the shallow loch — upper margin of the pine forest up to 700 metres — red deer

on the slopes — more effects of glaciation — effects of fire.

Point 7   *Sheltered Bay.* Fine views — water plants — bladderworts — heaths on the bank — differences between ling, cross-leaved heath and bell heather — dark green fritillary — the peculiar 'roding' call that woodcocks make when patrolling their territories — wood ant nests.

Point 8   *Alder Tree.* Old Scots pine (270 years old) — dead trees — woodpeckers, crested tit — primroses and orchids — *Sphagnum* moss — roe deer — common birch polypore fungus on old birch.

Point 9   The history of the castle and its ospreys — jackdaws — the reserve.

E. *The addresses of Wardens and other background information.*

Fig. 20. Loch an Eilein in the Cairngorms National Nature Reserve

No doubt, in the long-term, the effectiveness of the management of most reserves will depend on the number of paid and voluntary Wardens who can do this kind of work, while at the same time it may depend on the funds available for putting the Wardens' management suggestions into action. This may entail large capital expenditure for roads, car parks, camp sites, washing facilities and lavatories, but, in addition, we would do well to copy the Americans' example and spend money on providing proper Information Centres and museums so that the visitor can not only know something of what he may hope to see in an area, but understand how this can be achieved without spoiling the situation both for others and for the wildlife itself.

5 The local nature reserve

Regrettably perhaps, the Local Nature Reserve figures least of all in the mind of the public. These areas seldom involve great stretches of magnificent country, though occasionally they hold special species that catch the interest. The whole point of such a reserve is that it should be set up and managed by local interest and labour and should only depend on the Nature Conservancy for advice and occasional assistance. For financial if no other reasons it is unlikely that Local Nature Reserves will be large; usually there will only be a few acres that are known to be 'good' and which for various reasons, such as drainage and steepness of the land, are economically unsuitable for agriculture. These areas have often been leased from the owners at small rents. Increasingly, however, during the last few years the County Councils have been obtaining land for public recreation as open spaces. Frequently these larger areas include smaller units suitable for a reserve of some sort. The establishment and management of such sanctuaries with the financial backing of the Councils concerned, are a really viable trend in conservation and one which is bound to bring more public attention to the conservation movement.

Because of their relatively small size and easy access, Local Nature Reserves are particularly suited to management by schools. Many school courses involve project work and this can often be carried out in a practical and useful way on such reserves.

A school reserve

One such reserve is the Winchester College Nature Reserve named 'Fallodon' after Viscount Grey of Fallodon, a former member of the school (Figs 21 and 22). This small, 12,000 m² fenland reserve was set up in 1936 to provide a sanctuary for wild-life in an area of water meadows in the Itchen valley at Winchester in Hampshire. Unfortunately the area was fenced in to prevent grazing and this had the effect of allowing the growth of the nettles that were then able to thrive on the rich fenland soil. In 1951 reclamation work was started. However, as is so often the case, preliminary surveys were only superficially carried out and revealed a moderately interesting range of birds such as reed buntings and warblers that throve in the reeds and fenland vegetation, but little of botanical interest. The management policy was directed towards four main ends: 1. To improve drainage to prevent flooding and create interesting ditches and margin effects, where one range of habitat conditions gives way to another. 2. To control the nettles which effectively prevented anyone using the reserve. 3. To cut paths and construct bridges so that the reserve could be used with minimum disturbance to the community. 4. To diversify the habitat and create more niches for birds by planting fenland trees and shrubs and so producing a wooded fen or carr community.

The drainage scheme simply involved the opening up of the old ditches, digging out the mud and, where possible, allowing a flush of fast water through them to prevent further silting up. Some ditches were left static, partly to provide a contrasted habitat. Nettles are controlled every year by spraying with a dilute solution (55 g/l) of sodium chlorate which scorches the nettles but leaves the grasses

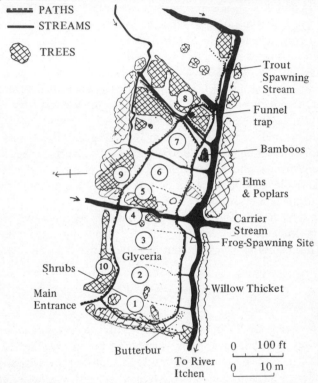

PATHS
STREAMS
TREES

Trout Spawning Stream

Funnel trap

Bamboos

Elms & Poplars

Carrier Stream

Frog-Spawning Site

Willow Thicket

Glyceria

Shrubs

Main Entrance

Butterbur

To River Itchen

0   100 ft

0   10 m

Fig. 21. The Fallodon Nature Reserve, Winchester. A small area of fenland managed as an educational reserve

more or less unaffected. Cutting also helps but the disturbance caused could upset the community, particularly at nesting time. It has also been suggested that removal of the nettles reduces the population of small tortoiseshell (*Aglais urticae*) and peacock (*Nymphalis io*) by removing their food plants, but enough nettles escape treatment to allow for a plentiful population of the butterflies.

Simple bridges of old sleepers and planks were made over the ditches and the paths kept open by cutting with sickles and mechanical scythes. There is no doubt that the use of such machinery disturbs the habitat but sporadic use is probably justified if the main nesting season can be avoided. Some clearance is vital as the vegetation may grow to a height of six feet by late summer. Piles of the cut vegetation are also useful for encouraging invertebrates such as beetles and spiders.

Planting schemes are always interesting as they involve a constructive rather than a destructive approach. Attempts were made to improve the diversity of plant life at tree, shrub and herb levels. In such planting schemes it would be a mistake to plant exotic types and it would possibly be unwise to bring in rare local species, at least in the first instance. This may endanger the plant in its natural habitat and until the autecology and requirements of the species are understood, there is too great a chance of failure. Occasionally, however, a special rescue operation may have to be carried out when a rarity is endangered by some development such as road-building.

Fig. 22. The Fallodon Nature Reserve

Often it is better to plant distinct or improved forms that are related to our wild species. Fenland supports willows and poplars extremely well and fast-growing species such as the cricket bat willow (*Salix alba subspecies coerulea*), balsam poplar (*Populus trichocarpa*) and alder (*Alnus glutinosa*) were planted to good effect. All these larger species provided good roosting for birds such as the blackbird.

Shrubs were planted in quite a variety under the tree cover. Apart from their aesthetic quality, these were chosen to provide nesting sites, flowers to attract insects and berries to provide autumn bird food. Various hawthorns (*Crataegus monogyna* and *C. carreri*), *Sorbaria* species, *Buddleja davidii*, *Cotoneaster salicifolia* and bamboos (*Phyllostachys*) were all tried with conspicuous success, though it could be argued that many of these are too unnatural for this habitat. Natural willows (*Salix purpurea, S. viminalis*) increased considerably both of their own accord and from cuttings which root very easily.

Table 11 Bird census in the Fallodon Nature Reserve. 1953–1957.

Weekly counts are carried out by a ¾-hr. walk around the Reserve. The results given are those obtained from a single walk in each case.

	28 May 1953	2 June 1955	2 June 1957
Sedge Warbler	8	4	4
Willow Warbler	5	0	0
Mistle Thrush	2	0	0
Song Thrush	2	5	4
Blackbird	2	8	4
Sparrow	0	0	5
Chaffinch	2	2	3
Reed Bunting	1	2	2
Mallard	3	0	0
Pheasant	1	0	0
Partridge	2	0	0
Starling	0	0	3
Blue Tit	1	0	5
Great Tit	1	0	1
White Throat	1	0	1
Grey Wagtail	1	0	0
Cuckoo	1	0	0
Robin	0	2	0
Wren	0	1	4
Greenfinch	0	4	0
Goldfinch	0	3	0
Jackdaw	0	0	2
Mute Swan	0	0	1
TOTAL	33	31	39
SPECIES	15	9	13

Herbs are particularly difficult to introduce or encourage in this highly competitive habitat. Few introductions did well apart from butterbur (*Petasites japonicus*) which is able to compete well with its vast spreading leaves. However, more success was achieved with increasing resident herbs. Marsh marigold (*Caltha palustris*) was increased by division of the clumps and planted successfully alongside the ditches. Comfrey (*Symphytum officinale*) grows from broken up chunks of its enormous roots. This is a particularly interesting species, not only on account of the colour variation in its flowers but also because it is food for the caterpillar of the scarlet tiger moth (*Panaxia dominula*), the local population of which has increased considerably over the years.

Less than ten years after the reclamation scheme had started, the main management aims had been achieved and the area was visually much more attractive, and held a greater range of plant species, both natural and planted. Bird life increased greatly and mammal life was noticeably abundant. Though the small mammals had probably always been common in the reserve, it was now at last possible to see them.

At this time a number of surveys of the wildlife were conducted. On the plant side full species lists were made and an investigation into the factors determining the survival of three of the most common species — reed grass (*Glyceria maxima*), hairy willow herb (*Epilobium hirsutum*) and nettle (*Urtica dioica*). In this instance it was found that the height of the water table was the main factor appearing to control the distribution of these plants. Rather belatedly it might have been pointed out that the drainage of the area could have benefited the nettle.

Surveys of the bird population were carried out in a number of ways. A ¾-hour walk around the perimeter track, noting all the birds seen, heard or nesting, provides a simple and quite effective method for assessing the resident and migrant population. Results of this survey are illustrated (Table 11 and Fig. 23). Bird ringing was also introduced, partly to obtain a better idea of the local population and also by way of subscribing to the international investigations into bird migration. Funnel traps (see Fig. 24) and mist nets were used with great success and among the rarer birds recorded were siskin and brambling.

In a developing habitat like Fallodon nesting sites in old trees are rare and nest-boxes are a simple way in which some species such as the tits, redstarts and fly-catchers can be increased. Figure 25 illustrates a simple but effective design. Birds usually take some time to get used to nestboxes; these must be in place well before the nesting season and they should be put up at a density which suits both the species and habitat. Different hole sizes also suit different birds; suggested dimensions are given in Table 12 on p. 52.

Perhaps some of the most interesting information has been obtained in the observations on small mammals. In all, three surveys have been carried out. In 1965 Longworth traps (Fig. 13) were used to obtain a preliminary idea of the species present and their distribution within the area. More detailed work was carried out in the years 1967–69 and the list of species found is given in Table 13 on p. 52.

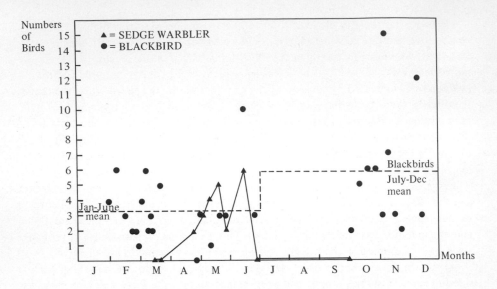

Fig. 23. *Blackbirds and Sedge warblers in the Fallodon Nature Reserve in 1954*

Fig. 24. *Funnel trap in the Fallodon Nature Reserve*

The larger mammals are much more rarely seen but the sighting of the otter is particularly interesting as this is a rare species in much of Hampshire, but the reserve is a suitable habitat with plenty of cover, trout in the streams and a good site for a holt under a fallen tree. In this instance the conservation measures seem to have paid off in an unexpected and satisfactory way.

The trapping programme for small mammals was carried out systematically over the area by saturating ten separate zones (see Fig. 21) with traps. To be able to assess the population it is necessary to mark the animals so that they may be recognised in

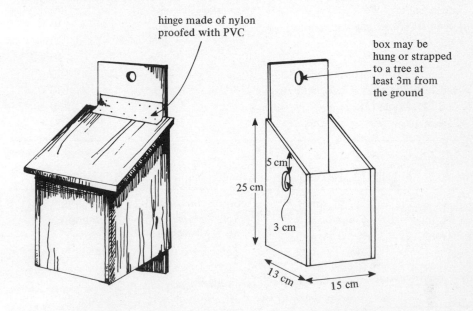

Fig. 25. Nestbox design suitable for many of the smaller birds. The PVC coated nylon is available from Thomas Foulkes, Department BO 70, Lansdowne Road, Leytonstone, London, E11

subsequent trapping and an idea of their movements also obtained. Marking of the common species can be carried out by toe clipping. Although this sounds a somewhat undesirable technique, it seems that the animals are virtually unaffected and suffer little pain if the toe is first anaesthetised with chloroethane. In any case advice as to the best technique should be obtained from a competent advisory body such as the British Museum (Natural History). Less satisfactory marking techniques involve fur clipping and the use of coloured dyes, but most of these methods are useless for a long-term trapping programme. Over the year it was possible to obtain a useful idea of the population density, range and movements of the commoner species; without a marking technique this would have been impossible.

Table 12 Birds that will nest in the nestbox illustrated in Fig. 25, modified for different hole size and depth.

(From *Cohen, E.,* Nestboxes, B.T.O. Field Guide No. 3, Third Edition (1961)).

	Entrance hole (mm)	Depth (mm)
Green Woodpecker (*Picus viridis*)	60	360
Green Spotted Woodpecker (*Dendrocopus major*)	50	300
Great Tit (*Parus major*)	27	130 +
Coal Tit (*P. ater*)	27	150 +
Blue Tit (*P. caeruleus*)	25	130 +
Nuthatch (*Sitta europaea*)	30	130 +
Redstart (*Phoenicurus phoenicurus*)	45	130 +
Pied Flycatcher (*Muscicapa hypoleuca*)	30	130 +
Tree Sparrow (*Passer montanus*)	28	160 +

Table 13 Mammals seen in Fallodon Nature Reserve 1967–69

A. Caught in Longworth traps	Pygmy shrew	*Sorex minutus*	Common
	Common shrew	*Sorex araneus*	Common
	Water shrew	*Neomys fodiens*	Rare
	Mole (young)	*Talpa europaea*	One only
	Bank vole	*Clethrionomys glareolus*	Common
	Short tailed vole	*Microtus agrestis*	Common
	Wood mouse (Fig. 26)	*Sylvaemus sylvaticus*	Very common
B. Observed in the area	Hedgehog	*Erinaceus europaeus*	Occasional
	Mole	*Talpa europaea*	Common
	Grey squirrel	*Neosciurus carolinensis*	Rare
	Water vole	*Arvicola amphibius*	Common
	Harvest mouse	*Micromys minutus*	One nest only found
	Brown rat	*Rattus norvegicus*	Occasional
	Stoat	*Mustela erminea*	Rare
	Otter	*Lutra lutra*	One young (c. 1 year old) seen

Fig. 26. Wood mouse in the Fallodon Nature Reserve

The results of part of this survey (1969) are given in the table below, which suggest that the small mammals may have a preference for the denser cover afforded by the trees and shrubs.

Table 14 Total numbers of small mammals caught in different habitats in the Fallodon Nature Reserve

Zone	1	2	3	4	5	6	7	8	9	10
Type of habitat	W/S	G	G	S/G	W	G	G	W/S	W	W
Numbers of small mammals caught	21	14	14	9	21	12	13	19	20	18

W = Dense tree cover.   2 nights trapping in each zone.
S = Shrubs and trees, fairly open.   25 traps per zone.
G = *Glyceria* meadow.

From extensive trapping and use of the capture-mark-recapture technique* it has

* The capture-mark-recapture technique The number of animals caught on any one day is recorded; these are all marked and then released. At least a day later, the animals are again sampled and the number of marked individuals in the total catch noted. The population is given by the following formula:

$$\text{Population} = \frac{(\text{No. caught on the first occasion} \times \text{No. caught on the second})}{\text{No. of recaptures}}$$

This technique is most suitable where large, rapidly re-assorting populations are being considered. Where, as in the case of small mammals, the animal may be either trap-shy or indeed use the trap as a well-established source of food, considerable caution is needed in interpreting the results.

also been possible to estimate the winter, spring, summer and autumn population of each of the commoner species. In 1969 about 90 specimens constituted the autumn population in the 12,000 m^2 reserve. It will be interesting to see if future surveys show any change in this population as conservation management proceeds. In the meantime it seems clear that planting shrubs and increasing the biological diversity of the area has in no way reduced the population, probably the reverse.

From this discussion of a school nature reserve it should be seen that there are infinite possibilities for applying conservation techniques and learning something of Natural History even though the area may be small in size. Although Fallodon is undoubtedly a rich and interesting area, there is no reason why equally interesting results should not be obtained from less attractive sites, even in urban areas. Indeed, it is in these that the unexpected and more exciting results are sometimes recorded.

A woodland reserve

Many reserves are of particular value, because they are showing interesting *clines* (gradations) in community or because they are in a state of succession or change. (*Succession* is the sequence of plants and animals that follows after the initial colonisation of an area.) The Fallodon Nature Reserve is one such example where the more interesting species are found around the margins of the ditches and in the developing wooded carr community. Woodland communities are then usually nearer the end of a succession; the community is more stable and approaching the climax situation. The interest in woodland reserves is usually on the aesthetic side, but there will be margins where interesting clines occur, not only along the edge of the wood, but surrounding paths and clearings. Small scale successions will also occur where a tree dies or is cut down. However, because the habitat has taken many years to develop and is of a more stable nature, it is much more difficult to modify it within a few years in any particular direction. This is in complete contrast to fens and marshes.

Ideally in every county there should be examples of the local woodland types conserved as reserves, but due to land costs this has seldom been achieved and most reserves tend to be on more marginal land. Nevertheless, as the various pressures on the countryside increase, the need for the establishment of such reserves, even though they may not, at least at first sight, appear to be of first-class natural history interest, becomes more and more vital.

An oakwood reserve

One such reserve is part of the 0·75 km^2 County Open Space area called Crab Wood near Winchester. A 0·12 km^2 portion of the open space has been designated a reserve and is managed by a representative of the local Wildlife Trust with help from local schools. In this instance it was possible to carry out an initial biological survey before any drastic management was begun. The survey was essentially of two types: the first a conventional listing of species of flowering plant, ferns, mosses and liverworts, of birds, moths, butterflies, small mammals and large mammals. These were recorded, where possible, on the map cards of the Biological Records Centre. The second was essentially a habitat survey which immediately suggested a number of conservation measures.

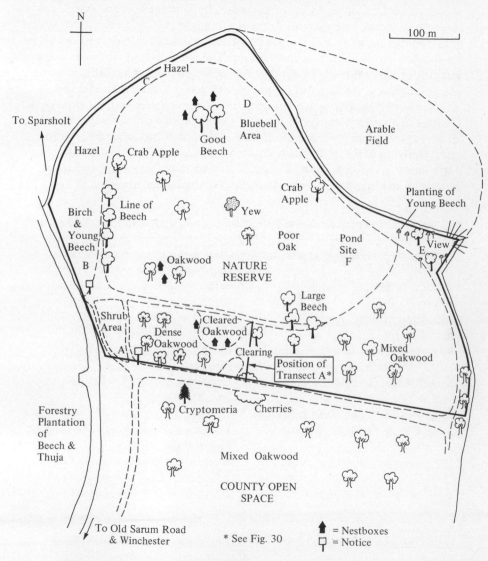

Fig. 27. Map of the Crab Wood Nature Reserve

The reopening of the perimeter track revealed (see map, Fig. 27) a series of differing habitats of interest.

Nearest the entrance (at A) there is an exceptional group of oakwood shrubs including hazel (*Corylus avellana*), spindle (*Euonymus europaeus*), dogwood (*Thelycrania sanguinea*), wayfaring tree (*Viburnum lantana*), guelder rose (*Viburnum opulus*) and privet (*Ligustrum vulgare*). All these provide nuts or berries in autumn which are useful food for birds and mammals. In parts these shrubs were rather overgrown, mainly with bramble, and it was thought that a clearance of the worst scrub, so that the more decorative and interesting shrubs could prosper, would be worthwhile. At the same time this clearance and bramble removal should encourage the ground flora, which, typically of a rich, moist clay soil was most interesting. Herbs common in this area include primrose (*Primula vulgaris*), wood spurge (*Euphorbia amygdaloides*), wood anemone (*Anemone nemorosa*), solomon's seal (*Polygonatum multiflorum*) and common spotted orchid (*Dactylorchis fuchsii*). The small-scale glades produced would probably favour butterflies and moths, particularly the Duke of Burgundy fritillary (*Hamearis lucina*), whose caterpillar feeds on the primrose and which is quite common in the area. More common butterflies and their food plants which also like this habitat are listed in Table 15.

Table 15 The more common butterflies in Crab Wood and their food plants

Speckled Wood (*Pararge aegeria*)	Grasses, e.g. Cocksfoot (*Dactylis glomerata*)
Meadow Brown (*Maniola jurtina*)	Grasses, e.g. Meadow Grass (*Poa pratensis*)
Small Heath (*Coenonympha pamphilus*)	Grasses, e.g. Dog's-tail Grass (*Cynosurus cristatus*)
Ringlet (*Aphantopus hyperanthus*)	Grasses, e.g. Cocksfoot (*Dactylis glomerata*)
Large Skipper (*Ochlodes venata*)	Grasses, e.g. Yorkshire Fog (*Holcus lanatus*)
Small Skipper (*Thymelicus sylvestris*)	Grasses, e.g. Lop-grass (*Bromus mollis*)
Small Copper (*Lycaena phlaeas*)	Docks, e.g. Red-veined Dock (*Rumex sanguineus*)
Brimstone (*Gonepteryx rhamni*)	Buckthorn (*Rhamnus catharticus*) and Alder Buckthorn (*Frangula alnus*)
Large White (*Pieris brassicae*)	Crucifers, e.g. Hedge mustard (*Sisimbrium officinale*)
Small White (*Pieris rapae*)	Various Crucifers
Green-veined White (*Pieris napi*)	Crucifers, e.g. Jack-by-the-Hedge (*Alliaria petiolata*)

Further round the track (at B) a group of birch (*Betula pendula*) suggested a change of emphasis (see Fig. 28). Removal of scrub and the least-good specimens of birch revealed regenerating beech and a ground flora composed of abundant twayblade (*Listera ovata*). Emphasis on the birch habitat should encourage species

Fig. 28. Birches in the Crab Wood Nature Reserve

associated with this tree from moths such as the buff-tip (*Phalera bucephala*), whose caterpillar feeds on the leaves, to the fly-agaric fungus (*Amanita muscaria*) which lives in a mycorrhizal association with the roots of the birch.

The next stand (C) is a dull one, being composed almost exclusively of old hazel (*Corylus avellana*) with no ground flora at all. This is a relic of the days when hazel coppicing was practised for fencing and other purposes. There is some historical interest in such a community when properly managed and it is hoped to clear about 2,000 m² each year so that a fourteen-year coppicing cycle will eventually be achieved. This will provide a man-determined succession which should enhance the species variety of the area.

The interest value of the stand that follows is mainly the magnificent bluebells (D) which, rather unusually, grow to the very bases of the beech trees. This is probably because the soil in Crab Wood is a light but moist clay and also because the beech canopy is not closed and enables the bluebells to survive despite their high light requirement. In the autumn and winter, traces of the activity of larger mammals

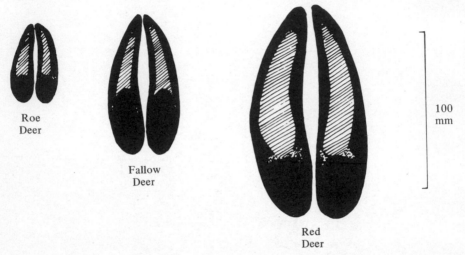

Roe Deer

Fallow Deer

Red Deer

100 mm

Fig. 29. Deer slots: right foreleg tracks of deer

in the area can be seen; badgers often dig up bluebell bulbs and their tracks can be followed to the edge of the wood where their fur may be left in any barbed-wire fence. Squirrels often use old stumps to sort and crack open their hazel nut collections. More rarely the activity of deer, principally roe, but also fallow may be seen. They may browse the bark from young trees and also leave their slots and tracks in the rides (Fig. 29).

The north-eastern part of the wood is rather less interesting, though there are some fine views of the local countryside and a small area here has been cleared to give a better view (E). The few good beech trees hereabouts have also been reinforced by planting with young replacements, and aerial layerings taken of the two remaining crab apple trees.

In spaces where many of the better trees had been cut down it was decided to create a new niche by constructing a small pond (F). There is no open water for some kilometres and it is hoped that this will increase the numbers of birds and mammals. Careful observation over the years will be needed to check the effect of this scheme.

In the southern part of the reserve there are 40,000 m² of comparatively good quality woodland. An extensive survey of this area was carried out by two methods. First, a sequence of aerial photographs were taken from a low-flying helicopter. Second, a survey party walked a series of transects, 25 metres apart, the length of the section. Any tree within 5 metres either side of the transect line was marked and its height and quality noted (Fig. 30). By comparing these sets of data it was

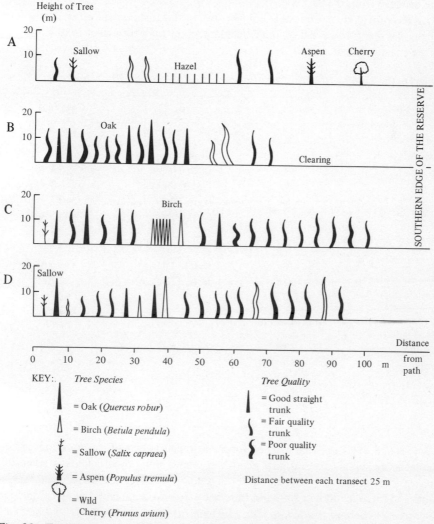

Fig. 30. Tree survey of Crab Wood: a series of line transects

possible to suggest a management policy. One area of about 8,000 m^2, adjacent to the central path, was clearly good oak, worthy of being made a special feature. Accordingly all the shrub layer, principally senescent hazel and bramble, was cut out. A few 1½-metre oaks were planted in the gaps and nest boxes attached to a number of trees.

The siting density and type of nest boxes was carefully considered and two trial groupings were made. Five were placed in this cleared area, and twelve boxes were placed approximately 25 metres apart in thick, uncleared and undisturbed oakwood some distance from the first site.

This has provided an interesting comparison; in this instance the actual density of the boxes seems to have been much less important than the effect of disturbance and the cover available. (See Table 16.)

Table 16 *The effect of siting of nestboxes on nesting success in Crab Wood (1970)*

Site	No. of Box	Species	Eggs laid
Undisturbed	1	—	—
oakwood	2	Blue Tit	8
with shrubs	3	Blue Tit	4 +
	4	Great Tit	8 +
	5	Blue Tit	11 +
	6	Great Tit	10 +
	7	Blue Tit	12
	8	Blue Tit	14
	9	Great Tit	some
	10	Blue Tit	some
	11	?	Half built, then deserted
Cleared oakwood	12	Nuthatch	4
near path	13	—	—
	14	Blue Tit	some
	15	—	—
	16	Blue Tit	some

A problem that has often worried conservationists is that of introductions. A number of local plants occur quite near Crab Wood, many of which are in some danger through road widening and other depredations. It has been suggested that a number of these could be planted in this cleared oakwood area. Such plants include the stinking hellebore (*Helleborus foetidus*) and the green hellebore (*H, viridis*), the lily-of-the-valley (*Convallaria majalis*) and the more common early purple orchid

(*Orchis mascula*). It has often been argued that such plantings might upset the community and create an unnatural garden-like image in a wild and natural habitat. However, few habitats in Britain, let alone Crab Wood, can be regarded as natural and, in view of the continuous loss of interesting species through the activities of man, I believe that such introductions are very useful, provided they are carried out with proper, expert advice and efficient records kept as to the resulting growth of the species.

A rather ordinary area like Crab Wood can, if properly managed, become an area of considerable aesthetic value and natural history interest. It is an excellent example of a Local Nature Reserve which can be looked after by local enthusiasts, supported by locally-raised funds, and can provide a useful amenity area quite near to a population centre.

6 Conservation of the single species

It is often said that if the habitat is looked after properly the species will look after themselves. While this generalisation is probably true it is liable to induce rather a negative approach to conservation. For one thing the environment may alter and induce a less satisfactory condition in the community; for another it has little regard for species of special interest. In some circles the conservation of rarities is frowned upon; certainly it should not be the be all and end all of conservation. However, deliberate protection of rarities and species in danger of extinction not only catches the public eye but also suggests specific policies that are all too often overlooked at the habitat level. It may also be implied that the conservation of single species is easier; this appears to be so because the aim is simpler and the factors affecting the species are more easily grasped. But it is not only rarities that can be conserved in this way; many farming policies are essentially single species management techniques. This is also true of many freshwater fishing policies, where both habitat conservation and fish culture come under the general heading of Fishery Management.

A trout fishery

Many British trout fisheries have been skilfully managed for years to conserve stocks of game fish such as trout and salmon. On the River Itchen, a Hampshire chalk stream (Fig. 31), survey of both habitat and fishing yields has gone along with management policies for some years.

Success of trout in the river must depend on a combination of all the following habitat factors:

(1) Good quality water
(2) Sites for reproduction
(3) Sites where the young can shelter
(4) Food for the young
(5) Sites where the adults can shelter
(6) Food for adults
(7) Freedom from competitors and predators
(8) Freedom from parasites

Each of these factors was examined and in some cases specific action taken. At the same time the yield of the fishery in terms of numbers and weight of fish taken, as well as their growth rate, was carefully recorded.

Brown trout like relatively cool water (the upper lethal temperature for young trout is about 16°C, though older trout can live at much higher temperatures nearer 23°C). At these higher temperatures the water should be completely saturated with oxygen, though at lower temperatures reduced saturation can be tolerated. The water should also be free of chemical pollutants such as detergents, pesticides and salts of heavy metals (see page 6).

It is unlikely that water quality is a limiting factor to the trout population in the river Itchen. Whilst a certain amount of treated sewage effluent is allowed into the river, the oxygen saturation is high at most times of the year due to the active growth of underwater plants such as water buttercup (*Ranunculus aquatilis*) which may raise the percentage saturation as high as 130 per cent in summer, though, because the solubility of oxygen in water is so low, this represents only 9·7 cm^3 oxygen per litre of water at 12°C. At the present time there is no evidence of pollution from chemical substances of any kind.

Reproduction is rightly regarded as the most critical phase in the life cycle of most species. If a species is rare, this is perhaps more often due to reproductive failure than anything else; yet over-effective reproduction, resulting in an over-dense

Fig. 31. The River Itchen at Winchester

population in which competition for food is serious, may also be disastrous. Surprisingly perhaps, few fishery managers make a serious effort to balance the reproductive potential of a fishery with the final crop. On a middle or lower reach of a river reproduction of trout is usually too low, while on higher, faster and more gravelly stretches reproduction may be high or even too high. On the Winchester stretch of the Itchen the former is the case and conservation measures have consisted in reopening and improving the water flow in a number of small streams or carriers that flow into the main river. Large numbers of trout and salmon use these recently developed streams for spawning in December and January each year. Both salmon and trout like swift (0·75 m/sec.) streams with gravel bottoms for cutting their redds. (Redds are holes, often more than half a metre deep, in which spawning can take place (Fig. 32).)

The alevins (young fish) wriggle out of the redds in about April and, as the food in their yolk sacs is nearly absorbed, begin to feed, as fry, on minute animal and

63

plant food. Clearly their habitat requirements will be quite different from those of the more mature fish and they will be particularly prone to predations from carnivorous fish such as the miller's thumb (*Cottus gobio*). Small streams, perhaps with a less powerful current, are more likely to satisfy their habitat requirements than the larger streams, but as they grow beyond yearling size (about 0·2 m) they will mostly migrate to the main river and exploit the different food that is available, as the large fish are removed by angling.

The problem of territory is an important one at this stage. Like most animals, a trout adjusts its position in the habitat so that it can obtain the food it needs and also any shelter or protection from man or other predators such as pike and heron. A single fish often dominates a certain 'run' or 'lie' between two weed beds; if the

Fig. 32. A salmon on a redd in a shallow stream

fish is caught it is frequently replaced remarkably quickly by another moving into the niche. Observation of the Itchen has suggested that there is a great deal of food, principally shrimps (*Gammarus pulex*) and the nymphs of various mayflies. It would seem likely that one of the main factors determining the abundance of fish in a chalk stream may well be the number of suitable territories. Management, by skilful weed-cutting, groyne construction and flow control, may be able to increase the numbers of such niches considerably (Fig. 33).

Competition is another important aspect and one which often arouses considerable controversy, usually due to lack of knowledge. Competition for breeding sites at the redds may be important and the salmon has come into disrepute here as he may dig over trout redds. Some years ago salmon used to be illegally removed from trout streams to prevent this but, in view of the danger that that species is now in, such action would be strongly deprecated. In addition there is evidence that the salmon,

naturally enough, prefers deeper water with a larger gravel size for the construction
of its redds. Trout are often seen hanging behind a salmon redd, perhaps more intent
on eating salmon eggs than on the construction of their own redds.

The grayling (*Thymallus thymallus*), which was, unfortunately, introduced into
the chalk streams a century or so ago, is probably a more serious competitor of trout
in the main river. It certainly feeds on much the same food and, particularly when
in a shoal, may bully the trout out of a given territory. Management usually involves

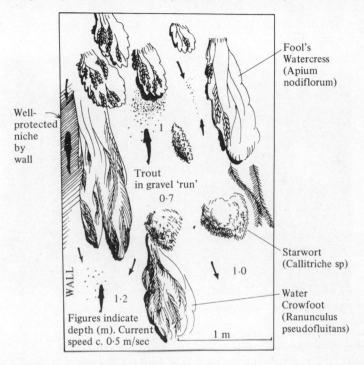

Fig. 33.   Trout territories in the River Itchen

either netting or electric fishing to remove such competitors and also to remove
predators (see below). Electric fishing is normally carried out from a boat (Fig. 34)
which has on board a D.C. generator producing about 15 amps. Two positive
electrodes are attached to the boat and two negative, paddle-like electrodes are held
by the fisherman. The fish are attracted to the negative from about 3 metres;
the larger the fish the more strongly it is attracted. Grayling and other unwanted
fish are then netted out, but trout are allowed to swim away by removing the
electrode and so cutting the current. Electric fishing is usually carried out after the
fishing season has ended, in early October, before the river becomes full and dirty
with winter rains.

Predators may attack trout at almost any stage in their lives. Spawning trout are often attacked by heron; alevins and fry by miller's thumb and stone loach; young trout by the older fish and almost any by the top carnivore, pike. These create havoc in a fishery. On a mile of Itchen over a hundred pike averaging 1·5 kg may be removed by electric fishing and with rod and line in a year; they may well have eaten more trout than were caught by all the trout fishermen. A rigorous watch on the river has to be maintained to keep check of predators such as pike, but heron represent more of a problem. These are protected birds and cannot be shot; like the otter, most fishermen would prefer to see them by the river, even at the expense of the loss of a few fish.

Fig. 34. Electric fishing

Leaving aside man as the arch predator for the moment, there is the final problem of parasites. The recent outbreaks of U.D.N. (Ulcerated Dermal Necrosis) on salmon and trout have emphasised not only how little is known about many parasites, but also how little we can do to control them. Trout are attacked by a number of external and internal parasites, some of which do little harm; others, particularly in combination or succession, may either debilitate or kill the fish. The table below lists some of the more important external and internal parasites that have been recorded on trout. Even though there may be well over a hundred 10–20 mm gut parasites in a specimen, most of these fish are in good condition. It is even tempting to suggest that the healthier the fish the more parasites it contains. The question that might be asked though is how much *healthier* it might have been if no parasites were present.

Infection by parasites will depend on a large number of factors; the genetic resistance of the trout, any acquired resistance, the health of the fish, other fish carrying the parasite into the river and alternative hosts such as birds bringing in

Table 17 Parasites found on trout

Type of Parasite	Species	Notes
ECTOPARASITES	Leech (*Piscicola*)	Usually only attacks senescent fish, particularly around gills.
	White spot or 'ich' (*Ichthyophthirius*)	A protozoan that frequently appears on fish brought into aquaria.
	'Pop-eye' fluke (*Diplostomulum*)	Not recorded at Winchester but increasing over Britain (1969) to serious proportions. Causes blindness due to cataract. Has a complex life cycle which also involves sea-gulls and snails.
	Gill flukes (*Discocotyle* and *Gyrodactylus*)	Not recorded at Winchester.
	U.D.N. (Ulcerated Dermal Necrosis) Fungus (*Saprolegnia*) and probably virus and slime bacteria	*Saprolegnia* often appears on salmon at spawning time and more rarely on trout. U.D.N., the most serious disease ever to have attacked salmon and trout, has not yet (1971) been recorded on the Itchen.
ENDOPARASITES	Spiny-headed worm (*Acanthocephala*)	Present in the lower gut of all Itchen fish, sometimes in great abundance (e.g. a 0·4 m trout contained 145). It does not appear to debilitate the host or lower the condition of the trout appreciably.
	Roundworms (*Agamonema*)	Quite often found in the gut and sometimes abundantly in the swim bladder.
	Tapeworms (*Eubothrium*)	Not recorded at Winchester.

larval stages of the parasite. Little can be done to prevent and control an outbreak other than by treating confined fish (e.g. in a stewpond) with compounds such as Malachite Green which reduce fungi and bacteria. Once an outbreak of a serious disease such as U.D.N. has occurred, the best long-term answer must be to select immune fish and breed from them in hatchery conditions in the hope of producing genetically immune stock. As yet this seems to have been practised relatively little.

I have dealt with parasites rather fully, not only because of their topical importance but also because they emphasise how much basic biology is needed in terms of identification, life-cycle study and breeding if a fishery is to cope with a serious infection.

Finally, trout conservation must, beyond all else, depend on fishing intensity, yet it is remarkable how little effort is made on many fisheries to gauge the fishing to suit the natural productivity of the river. A fishery is judged as good if plenty of large fish are caught, yet how rarely is any effort made to assess the growth rate of fish? Frequently too many young, undersized fish are left in the water and only old, large fish removed. In some cases too many large fish may be removed so that spawning stocks may be depleted. The frequent remedy for lack of fish is to stock with yearling or mature fish, yet it has been demonstrated over and over again that there is no point in filling a river with fish when there is insufficient food or when all the territories are filled. Such a policy is disastrous as all the fish may lose condition in the ensuing competition. Stocking is usually only desirable in new waters or where little reproduction is possible due to lack of gravelly spawning streams, or finally where angling intensity is so high that few adult fish are present. Management policy must therefore include an understanding of the age and growth rate of the trout if catches are to be properly regulated and, perhaps most important of all, the information obtained may indicate whether effective management techniques are being employed. If data in the register of fish caught is carefully analysed, it will usually give most of the information needed. Such data should include both the length and weight of the fish, and the condition of the fish is got from the expression:

$$K = \text{approx. } 1 \cdot 0 = \frac{1000 \times \text{wt in pounds}}{0 \cdot 427 \times \text{length in inches}^3} = \frac{\text{wt in g}}{\text{length in m}^3}$$

A well-conditioned fish may have a K factor of over $1 \cdot 0$, perhaps as high as $1 \cdot 3$, and a poorly-conditioned fish will have a K factor below $1 \cdot 0$.

With regard to the age of fish, few fisherman care to say at a glance what is the age of a single specimen. Trout spawn around Christmas time and hatch in April to grow to about 5 oz (138 g) during their first year. In the Itchen they will have roughly doubled their weight by May of their second year, to weigh about 11 oz (312 g). This information can be obtained by netting an area and finding the numbers centering about a particular weight. The fisherman's sample begins at higher weights but can again be used if the catch within a narrow period of time

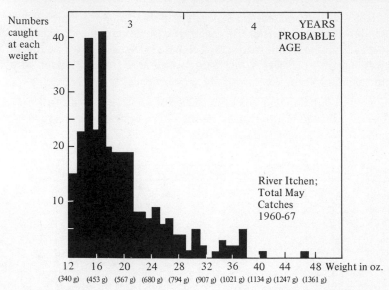

Fig. 35. Trout catch in the month of May; numbers caught at different weights

(e.g. the month of May) (Fig. 35) is examined. This suggests that a large number of the fish caught by Itchen fishermen are three-year-olds and that few live beyond four years. A typical life-story might work out as follows:

Dec. 1966	May 1967	May 1968	May 1969	May 1970	May 1971
Spawned	Hatched	5 oz 142 g	11 oz 312 g	16 oz 453 g	36 oz 1021 g
		↑ 1 Year Old	↑ 2 Years Old	↑ 3 Years Old	↑ 4 Years Old

The wide variation in weight and length for these fish is given in the table below:

Table 18 The Relationship between Age, Weight and Length of Itchen Trout (in the month of May)

Age	Weight		Length	
	oz	g	in	m
2	c. 11	c. 312	c. 11	c. 0·28
3	12–28	340–799	12–15	0·30–0·39
4	29–c. 50	800–1400	16–c. 18	0·40–0·46

If these age, weight and length relationships are accepted for Itchen fish at Winchester, then the numbers of fish caught at each age group each year can be calculated and the trends in fishery crop compared (Fig. 36). If we assume a constant fishing pressure, several interesting points arise from this graph which illustrate the importance of such work to fishery management:

(1) The trout population was small and stable for some years prior to 1963.
(2) A change occurred in 1963 which resulted in a progressive increase in both numbers of fish caught and size of fish.

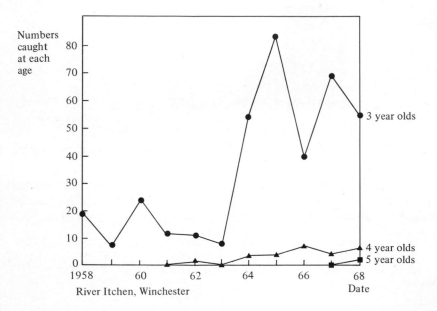

Fig. 36. Changes in a fishery crop; numbers of trout at different ages caught in May each year

(3) This change may have begun two or more years previously when the fish were spawned.
(4) The change may also be due to a better trout habitat in terms of food and territory.

During 1964 it was suggested that too many young three-year-old fish were being caught. The graph indicates that this is not so as the numbers of four- and five-year-olds continues to rise in 1965 and 1966. Management policies from 1958 onwards had concentrated on improvement of spawning streams and so it is likely that this paid off some years later after the communities in these streams had had a chance to re-establish themselves. At the same time removal of competitors and

70

predators by electric fishing was practised for the first time. These two modifications to the habitat have caused a three-fold increase in the yield of trout with only slight stocking and illustrate how deliberate conservation of one species may be successfully practised, even though it may have taken five years or more to reap the benefits.

The osprey story

It might be fitting to end this account of conservation of single species by mentioning one of the most famous success stories in British conservation — that of the osprey.

Fig. 37. An osprey bringing in a fish for its young

Many species that are apparently in danger in a certain area may be in such a state because they are on the limits of their usual distribution zone. Although ospreys (Fig. 37) have bred through much of the northern hemisphere, their breeding areas in Europe at the present time are in Russia, Finland, Sweden and Norway and there is some indication that they are spreading more to the west, particularly when on migration from their breeding sites in these countries towards their winter feeding grounds around the Mediterranean. These casual migrants may be responsible for re-establishing the breeding colonies in Scotland.

Ospreys bred fairly frequently in Speyside in the nineteenth century and breeding pairs nested and quite often raised young around the famous loch at Eilein Castle, but over the first half of the twentieth century they were frequently disturbed by tourists and egg-collectors. There is no certain record of a pair nesting successfully.

Although migrants were seen from time to time, ospreys were sighted more and more frequently around Speyside in the early 1950's and even observed fishing for pike and trout in the lochs. An eyrie was constructed near Loch Garten in 1955 but the nest was eventually deserted and another so-called 'frustration' eyrie constructed elsewhere. In 1956 another nest was constructed and eggs were laid but once again the nest was abandoned, probably due to disturbance, as the eggs disappeared.

In 1958 the Royal Society for the Protection of Birds (R.S.P.B.) determined to prevent further disturbance and placed a continuous guard on the nest, but unhappily the eggs were once again removed and it was realised that, if the birds were not to be disturbed yet again, a more efficient guard system would have to employed. And so, in 1959, over 2·6 km^2 of the woodland surrounding the tree where the ospreys habitually tried to nest were declared a statutory bird sanctuary with no permitted access without permit. Great pains were taken to ensure that the eyrie was undisturbed; barbed wire was placed around the base of the tree and a well-concealed observation and guard hide constructed close by. A base camp was built to provide amenities for the reserve wardens. An efficient microphone system was arranged, partly to listen to sounds made by the birds and also to detect any intruders. All these preparations and precautions paid off and there was great excitement at the hide when, on 8th June, the first chirpings of a newly hatched chick were heard.

Inevitably large numbers of ornithologists wished to see the birds in their eyrie and the R.S.P.B. took the bold decision of building a public observation hide. This would satisfy both ornithologists and the public in general and also provide useful publicity.

The success of this venture was quite staggering and in the six weeks while the chicks were being raised 14,000 visited the observation hide. By the middle of August the three young ospreys and their parents began to disperse from the area of Loch Garten. During the ten years from 1959 to 1968 a total of eighteen young were fledged at the Loch Garten eyrie in spite of nests being destroyed by gales on two occasions. See table opposite. At the same time other ospreys, maybe some of them locally-raised birds, attempted to nest at other sites in Speyside and, although in some cases the eggs failed to hatch due most probably to the traces of chlorinated hydrocarbons (D.D.E.) found in them, some successful breeding has taken place.†

And so, even though man has helped the osprey re-establish itself in Britain, largely by preventing the activities of the egg-collector, he may, once again, be

† An excellent film 'Operation Osprey' is available from the Royal Society for the Protection of Birds, The Lodge, Sandy, Bedfordshire.

Table 19 Ospreys at the Loch Garten Eyrie, Speyside, Scotland

Year	1st egg laid	Number fledged	Number of visitors to the hide
1959	1st May	3	14,000
1960	28th April	2	20,000
1961	29th April	3	21,500
1962	1st May	1	23,000
1963	25th April	Nest and eggs destroyed in gale	14,000
1964	23rd April	3	26,000
1965	16th April	1	23,000
1966	16th April	Nest and eggs destroyed in gale	19,500
1967	17th April	3	26,000
1968	16th April	2	37,500
1969	15th April	2	39,500
1970	18th April	3	39,500
Total in 11 years		23	303,500

By the courtesy of the Royal Society for the Protection of Birds

putting the future of these magnificent birds in a state of jeopardy by pollution. Insecticides which accumulate in the fish which are themselves high up the food chain, may reach lethal proportions in the bird-of-prey. It is in trying to prevent or control this sort of gross upset of our natural environment that the importance of the world-wide conservation movement lies.

Footnote: In spite of all the measures and precautions taken, the 1971 clutch of eggs were stolen from the Loch Garten eyrie.

Index

72
74
75
76
77
79
81
83
85
88